WHO
Do You Say
I AM

WHO Do You Say I AM

An intimate conversation with the Only Begotten Son

DANNY CLIFFORD

HEART AND SOUL MINISTRIES

Printed in the United States by **IngramSpark**

The author guarantees all contents are original and do not infringe upon the legal rights of any other person or work.

Portions of this book may be used in and reproduced with the permission of the author and or publisher Danny and or Michelle Clifford. Contact us at http://www. heartandsoulministriesinc.com

Bible quotations are noted.

ISBN Number: 978-0-578-17086-2

Cover Design by: Award-Winning Graphic Designer Lisa Hainline **LIONSGATE Book Design**, *LionsgateBookDesign.com*

Interior Designed and Formatted by: **Steve Plummer, spdesign@hargray.com**

Book Edited by: **Frank W. Kresen/proof positive frankkresen@hotmail.com**

EDITOR'S REVIEW

I T IS EVERY journalist's dream to land the assignment of interviewing an extremely famous (or infamous), influential celebrity or politician—especially if there has been controversy generated by the person's actions.

The BBC reporter David Frost interviewed Richard Nixon shortly after he had resigned as President of the United States. The interview was broadcast on television around the world, and it garnered some of the highest ratings ever recorded for a news show.

Other highly rated televised interviews of this type that come to mind are Barbara Walter's interview with Monica Lewinsky about her affair with President Bill Clinton and, more recently, Diane Sawyer's interview with Bruce Jenner shortly before the famous Olympic decathlete transitioned his gender to female.

But, here, in Danny Clifford's, *Who Do You Say I Am?* We encounter **The Luckiest Journalist in the History of the World**. His assignment is to interview none other than the Son of God Himself—Jesus Christ.

Clifford's engaging style draws the reader in, and the book becomes a sort of "Let me explain what went on behind the scenes and set the record straight" opportunity for Jesus to clarify—in plain, everyday language—some of the deepest, most enduring mysteries of all time: His own life and mission.

Christians the world over should enjoy this fascinating—if only imagined—sit-down session with the most influential human being who ever lived.

Editor Frank Kresen
Artisan/proof positive
frankkresen@hotmail.com
816 523 -6482

ACKNOWLEDGEMENTS

THANK YOU TO the armed guards and support personnel I served with at Camp Bondsteel, a United States military base located in the small Baltic country of Kosovo. I worked for a civilian company performing force protection security as an armed guard and supervisor for United States military personnel and other European countries' military armed personnel stationed at Camp Bondsteel.

Thank you and **God bless** all of you: Michael Adcock, Cory Allen, Daniel Clifford II, Miss Graham, Mike Jones, Corey Leadbetter, James Lee, Arvan Lettsome - KBR Foreman, Grant Liverett, Theo McShan, Brilliant Pitre, Gordon Pullen, my close friend Jerome Thompson, and, finally, a special "Thank you" to Pastor Bobby Bethea for his prayers and teachings while we served together in Kosovo.

These are some of the sheep whom God sent me to help them find and return to the Shepherd's Kingdom's Pen. Many of them gave their life to Jesus, while others re-dedicated their life to becoming Disciples of Christ. You all made this book come to life with your questions and desire to seek and know the one true God and His son Jesus.

Special acknowledgement to my son, Danny Clifford II, who on September 6, 2014, at midnight, gave his life to Jesus, and to his wife

Andrea, who also accepted Jesus as her Savior in the late summer of 2014.

I'd also like to acknowledge Carl Langston, a young man who God has changed from being a prisoner of Satan's worldly systems to a man who has given his life to Jesus and is learning how wonderful it is to have a relationship with God the Father.

We have watched Carl fall down and get back up as he is learning how important it is to be obedient to Jesus's teachings. I thank God for Carl's salvation and for being obedient to God's instruction to him. As I write this book, Carl is pursuing his dream of being a UFC fighter, and, one day soon, I believe he will be fighting for the Championship. Praise God for Carl's salvation and dedication.

REVIEWS

AnnaBella Ivanovska writes:

I have never read a book about God, so I thought I wouldn't like this book. But the moment I began to read it, I was captivated and knew that my generation desperately needed this book. It's not that we think God is bad or don't like God. No, that's not why. We need this book because were not taught **the truth** about Jesus and God; we simply don't know the real God at all.

Most of my friends believe in what people taught them and have done what they were told, but nothing is working. They feel alone, have no hope, and are lost. Most of them don't know God or the truth about Jesus. Others have lost their faith and trust in God.

After reading this book, I know God existed before creation, and I now know God created us to live a wonderful life and will never forget us, because He loves us. We need to be taught the truth about how to seek and find God through His Son Jesus. This book, *Who Do You Say I Am?* teaches us the truth about Jesus and His Father, God. My generation needs to read this book.

The part I like best in this book is when the author talks about souls. He talks about the body dying, but our soul lives on forever. The reason I like this so much is that my generation and I also believe that our soul lives on forever.

This book gave me a greater understanding of creation and why God the Father and Jesus created us. It inspired me to have faith in Jesus and establish a relationship with God. I have come to know that the one who gave us life is the one who gave His life for us. All I have to do is believe in Him. This is a very good book. Thank you for writing it, Mr. Danny Clifford.

ANNABELLA IVANOVSKA, 16 YEARS OLD, FROM KUMANOVO, MACEDONIA

Lanay Clifford writes:

Who Do You Say I Am? An Intimate Conversation With the Only Begotten is a wonderful conversation with Jesus as He shares with us that the way of living without fear in our life is by believing in who He is. God is the creator of all beings, and, as his children, we should all be respectful and make the world a peaceful and better place.

My generation needs this book because we do not appreciate and respect God. Many of my generation don't believe in God. We don't know or give a second thought as to how our beautiful world was created. We are void and empty inside, we lack something, and this book teaches us what we lack and how to receive it.

I really liked this book and recommend it to everyone. It shows you how to seek God for change, by allowing God to dwell in you; the results will be starting life over again with the kingdom of heaven living within you. Thank you, Grandpa, for sharing God's ways in his book, I like it and know it will help my generation.

LANAY CLIFFORD, 13-YEAR-OLD STUDENT FROM LONDON, ENGLAND

DEDICATION

THIS BOOK IS dedicated to my beautiful wife and best friend, whose prayers, encouragement, and love sustained me while we were separated for a year to accomplish God's mission in Kosovo. Michelle's strength and prayers kept me standing through the spiritual battles as Satan's forces tried to stop us and get us to quit.

In February 2015, while I was in Kosovo, Michelle had a growth removed that contained cancerous cells. The doctors scheduled her for a second operation on March 10, 2015, to search for additional cancer, but they found none, as Jesus had healed her totally. Her faith through the entire ordeal was like a rock—as she leaned on Jesus for total healing.

God has blessed me, allowing me to have such a gifted, beautiful woman as my wife, best friend, and lover. Thank you, Lord Jesus, for allowing me to be Michelle's husband.

This book is also dedicated to my grandchildren Tracy, Lanay, Brandon, and Gabriel-James, who will read this someday and understand the love, grace, and mercy that Jesus and Father God has for them, and they will believe in Him and serve Him.

CONTENTS

CHAPTER 1

THE ONLY BEGOTTEN SON

THE MOST CONTROVERSIAL person in the history of the world, without question, is **Jesus of Nazareth.** What makes Jesus so divisive is people not knowing and understanding His relationship to the human race and to His Father, the only true Most High God.

People all over the world want to know the truth about who Jesus really is. We want to know about heaven and how to attain heavenly status. We want to know **the truth** about creation, sin, the devil, the spiritual realm, and how we humans should treat God. We want to understand **why** the human race is going through so much suffering from famines, wars, sicknesses, diseases, destruction, and death.

So today, I have the honor of introducing you to a man that has done the impossible hundreds of times. He was born in Bethlehem in a manger, by way of eternity in Heaven. His mother's picture or statue is in every Catholic Church in the world. His Father is the Author of a Book that has been on the best-seller list since the beginning of time.

This man walked on water, turned water into wine, and fed 5000 hungry men with two fish and five loaves of bread and had 12 baskets of food left over. He raised every dead body he encountered back to life.

I introduce to you the **Son of Man,** who gave His life for you and me; He was raised from death's tomb back to life, never to die again. Instead, He ascended into heaven, where He now sits on His Father's throne.

Please welcome into your hearts and minds **Jesus of Nazareth,** the **Son of God,** and listen as He answers many of your questions in this intimate interview.

Journalist:

Jesus, when did you come to exist as the "Son of God"?

Jesus:

Although Christians usually say that I am the Son of God, only a few actually believe one of the most important truths about me. I pre-existed as the Son of God long before I was born in the flesh as the Son of Man through my virgin birth with Mary more than two thousand years ago.

My Father God is the only true God and the absolute source of all things. Everything originated from Him, including me. I am literally the Spirit Son of my Spirit Father God by spiritual birth.

I am unique in that I had a beginning before all creation. In Proverbs, the Bible says, "The Lord possessed me in the beginning, before he created anything else. From ages past, I am. I existed before the earth began. I lived before the oceans were created, before the springs bubbled forth their waters onto the earth, before the mountains and the hills were made. Yes, I was brought forth before God made the earth and fields and the first handfuls of soil. I was there when he established the heavens and formed the great springs in the depths of the oceans. I was there when he set the limits of the seas and gave them his instructions not to spread beyond their boundaries. I was there when he made the blueprint for the earth and oceans. I was the craftsman at his side. I was his constant delight, rejoicing always in his presence." (Proverbs 8:22-30 Living Bible TLB)

Journalist:

Jesus, will you explain what "only begotten son" means?

Jesus:

My Spirit birth can be compared with Isaac's human birth to Abraham and Sarah. Isaac was born as the second son, born of Abraham 14 years after Ishmael was born. However, Isaac was the only begotten son of his Father Abraham, because he was the only son my Father promised to Abraham.

You see, Isaac was born according to the Spirit, unlike the first son, Ishmael, who was born according to Sarah's plan. She arranged to have her Egyptian slave servant Hagar bear children through Abraham because she was getting too old to have children. (Galatians 4:28-31 and Genesis chapters 16 and 17.)

My Father spoke to Abraham when Ishmael was 13 years old and told him He would bless Sarah and give him a son from her! *I will bless her richly, and she will become the mother of many nations. Kings of nations will be among her descendants.* Abraham bowed down to the ground and laughed to himself in disbelief. "How could I become a father at the age of 100?" he thought. "And how can Sarah have a baby when she is 90 years old?"

Abraham asked My Father, "May Ishmael live under your special blessing!" My Father told Abraham, "**No!** Sarah, your wife, will give birth to a son for you. You will name him **Isaac,** and **I will confirm my covenant with him** and **his descendants** as an everlasting covenant. As for Ishmael, I will bless him also, just as you have asked. I will make him extremely fruitful and multiply his descendants. He will become the father of twelve princes, and I will make him a great nation. **But my covenant will be confirmed with Isaac,** who will be born to you and Sarah about this time next year." (Genesis 17 NLT)

So, as Isaac was the only begotten son of his Father Abraham, **I am the only begotten (promised) Son** of my Father, God.

As Isaac's human seed was in the body of his father Abraham before he could be born, my Spirit Seed was in my Spirit Father God before I was born. Of course, the difference between my birth and Isaac's birth is that Abraham needed a human wife, Sarah, for Isaac to be born, but my Father is Spirit, not a man; therefore, He did not need a spirit wife for me to be brought forth spiritually. (John 4:24)

"Begotten" is what God intended or promised. I am the only begotten Son of God, and Isaac was the only begotten son of Abraham. This is what my Father intended and promised.

Journalist:

Jesus, some people are confused with your claims to be the Son of God, the Son of Man, and also be God. Would you clarify the confusion? Are you truly the Son of God *and* God?

Jesus:

Let me address your three-part question by first answering the "Son of God part." As I explained, **I am** the **only begotten Son** born of my Spiritual Father, God, making me the Son of God.

Now let me address the second part of your question—one that has not been explained well, thus leaving many people confused, doubting, and puzzled. The question is, "How is it possible for me to be God, in the flesh?"

When I was born in the flesh from Mary my mother, who was impregnated supernaturally by my Father's Holy Spirit, I was born in the flesh as God's Son and/or the Son of God. Therefore, I am God in the flesh, but only as **God the Son.** I am a separate and subordinate God, always obedient to my Father, who is the only true and most High God.

My Father is *omniscient*—meaning He is unlimited in His knowledge, in His awareness, and in His understanding. He perceives all things.

He is also *omnipresent*—meaning He is present everywhere at the same time.

God, My Father, is *omnipotent*. He is called **"Almighty God"** because of His great, unlimited authority and power.

My Father is Spirit, and He brought me forth and made me just like Himself. I am Spirit, and I inherited all of His attributes and qualities. Like My Father, I am immortal, holy, righteous, loving, just, gracious, merciful, forgiving, and more.

However, I am not a co-equal God with my Father. My Father **is always greater than me,** as I sit at His right hand on our heavenly thrones.

My Father has put everything under my feet. Now when I say that "everything" is under my feet, this does not include My Father God. We function together in total harmony, in one accord. I am subordinate to My Father, always obedient and submissive to His Will.

In summary, I'll answer the third and final part of your question, "How and/or why am I the Son of Man?"

The Jewish people couldn't understand how I could be the Messiah, because I grew up and lived in Nazareth they assumed I was born in Nazareth. They also thought my step father Joseph was my actual father. So they referred to me as "son of man," meaning no way was I the Messiah, because I was the "son of a man."

However, there many others who called me the "Son of Man" and "Son of God." By this, they were showing respect for me, my Father's Only Begotten Son that He sent to Earth to be born of a human being—the "Son of Man." In human relations, I am your brother.

I became known as *the Word.* I was with God my Father in the beginning and I—*the Word, was God.* I already existed when you were created.

Then the Word, me, Son of Man, and Son of God became flesh and dealt among you. I AM God in the flesh—only as God's Son, sent to become Son of Man.

Everything My Father God created was created through me. I gave life to everything that was created, and my life brought light to everyone. John 1:1-4

When My Father wanted something accomplished, it became **His Will.**

What My Father God willed, I, the Word, spoke, and what the Word spoke, the Holy Spirit's power performed, accomplishing **My Father's will.**

Just to recap the question, "Am I God in the flesh?"

Yes, I am God manifest in the flesh. I am the Word that became flesh and dwelt among you. My Father, who is invisible to mortal eyes, is pleased to have all His fullness dwell in me and through me, to reconcile to Himself all things, whether things on earth or things in heaven, by making peace through my blood, shed on the cross, for you.

If you have seen me, you have seen the Father and heard the Father speak through me.

My Father loves you so much that He sent me, so that whoever would believe in me and obey my teachings would have everlasting life and live eternally with us.

Those who refuse to believe in me and my work, as Son of God, will die in their sins, condemned forever by my Father, because they **rejected me.**

Thank you for asking that three-part question. It's important to know and understand that I had a beginning and that I am my Father's Son. However, my Father has no beginning. He always was.

CHAPTER 2

IN THE BEGINNING

Journalist:

JESUS, I'D LIKE to shift topics and ask you about creation. Will you teach us the truth about the creation of Satan and the fallen evil angels? And why and how this happened?

Jesus:

Yes, I will start from the very beginning, and when I say from the beginning, I mean the beginning of creation.

After my Father gave spiritual birth to me, but before we created creation, my Father explained to me His detailed plan of creation—how and why He would achieve His vision of angels in the heavenly places. My Father's plan also included the creation of the universe and human beings, who would be sons and daughters of my Father, representing us on the planet we would create for you, Earth.

So, as God's only begotten Son, I inherited all of my Father's creative powers. Everything in the entire universe, all living and non-living things, were created by my Father **through me.** God created everything through me.

When my Father and I created angels, we created them as spiritual beings with intelligence, emotions, and a will. We created all the angels holy and righteous, with diverse shapes, sizes, names, and different responsibilities. They live with us in the height of heaven, performing worship and enjoying being around the glory of my Father and me.

We put one of the powerful Cherub angels we created in an exalted position right over the throne of the universe and named him Lucifer. We created Lucifer as the model of perfection, full of wisdom and exquisite in beauty. He was adorned with every precious stone beautifully crafted for him and set in the finest gold. We gave them to him on the day we created him.

We ordained and anointed him as the mighty angelic guardian. He had access to our holy mountain, and he walked among the stones of fire. Lucifer was blameless in all that he did until the day **evil was found in him.**

Everything created by my Father and me in the heavens, including angelic beings, was holy, righteous, and good, until **evil was found in Lucifer.**

Lucifer's pride caused him to devise a plan to ascend into heaven and exalt his own throne above the stars of God.

Lucifer accepted this plan in his heart:

> I will ascend to the heavens;
> I will raise my throne above the stars of God;
> I will sit enthroned on the mount of assembly, on the
>   utmost heights of Mount Zaphon.
> I will ascend above the tops of the clouds;
> I will make myself like the Most High.

After we created the earth, but before we created human beings, pride overcame Lucifer. His plan was to lead one-third of heaven's angels in an all-out assault and rule everything by forcibly taking control of my Father's throne.

Lucifer and his host of angels, who chose to disobey our structure of creation by assaulting my Father's throne, became evil and sinful angels, opposing my Father and me. My Father God and I are holy. It is impossible for us to exist with evil.

So, war broke out in heaven. Archangel Michael and his angels went to battle with the red dragon and his angels. Lucifer and his forces of evil angels were defeated, and there was no room for them in heaven any longer.

Lucifer was cast down and out of heaven. He and the evil, unclean angels, who supported him in his rebellion against God, were literally ejected from God's throne with all the quickness and power of lightning. They were cast down to planet Earth. They were confined and restrained to Earth and the atmospheric heaven around Earth, by the command of my and my Father's Word.

When Lucifer was cast out of heaven to Earth, he was never again called "Lucifer." He became the seducer—the deceiver of all humanity. His name changed. That age-old serpent became known by several other names, including the **Serpent, Satan,** meaning "the **Accuser,**" "the **Evil one,**" and "the **Devil.**" This all occurred before humanity was created.

Journalist:

You told us that you and God created Lucifer. In creating Lucifer, God must have created evil, correct?

Jesus:

No, my Father is incapable of creating evil. My Father and I are capable of creating only good. When we created the Earth, everything we created in and on earth was good.

We created Lucifer as a model of perfection, full of wisdom, righteous, holy, and with a free will to choose. Lucifer developed evil in his heart and then gave birth to evil. <u>He is the creator of evil</u>.

A war broke out in heaven between good and evil. Evil lost, so we cast Lucifer and his evil angels out of heaven to Earth. At that moment, both good and evil—Satan—existed on the Earth.

CHAPTER 3

CREATING HUMANS

Journalist:

J ESUS, THANK YOU for your explanation. Very interesting!

I would like to shift the topic to the creation of human beings. How did God create human beings?

Jesus:

My Father and I are Spirit, so we created humans to be like us, in our image. We created a **body** of flesh from the dust of the ground, holy and righteous, and breathed into the nostrils the breath of life, putting a piece of ourselves into humanity. At that very instant, **man,** Adam, became a living **spirit** being with a **soul.**

You are created with a **soul** that we destined at the time of creation to live with us forever. We gave you our Holy Spirit, at creation, with the purpose to communicate and guide you, through the spirit we put in you.

Then, we took a rib from the body of Adam and made the female. Adam named the female "woman." The **body** of flesh, which we created, contains and confines your spirit and soul, restricting you physically to one location at a time. The human body of flesh was created holy and righteous when we created Adam and Eve.

You were also created with many of our traits, for example, love, righteousness, holiness, goodness, kindness, joy, peace, and truthfulness. These are a short list of the many traits we gave you at creation.

So, you are much like us in many ways. A couple of major differences are that we created your body of flesh to confine the spirit that we gave you and to confine your soul, which is eternal. You were confined to one place at a time, on Earth.

Each one of you are created with different DNA in your body, making you separate, different, and unique individuals. You are not simply robotic beings.

We established guidelines and gave human beings the authority and dominion to reign over Earth. Adam and Eve were our representatives, our governors, representing us on earth.

My Father and I blessed the human race with the gift to reproduce other spirit beings. We did this so we could have holy, righteous children. Our intentions are that human children are to be birthed and raised within the parameters of marriage, as defined by me and my Father God.

One of the most important capabilities we gave you is a **free will.** We created you with an independent ability to **freely choose to do what you desire to do.**

We created you with the ability for your soul to choose freely to do what you want to do. Your soul is the real you. If you decide to go against our laws, structure, and commands of creation, **we must honor what you choose.** It is the way we created you, and we cannot go against our own structure and word.

Journalist:

Jesus, will you elaborate on how God designed and intended for us to function with our body, soul, spirit, and free will?

Jesus:

Thank you for asking this question. Many people have wondered or asked this question in their heart and mind.

In the beginning, we created you holy, righteous, and pure. You were incapable of thinking anything evil. There was no such thing as sin.

Your body is extremely sensitive to your physical surroundings and the natural things of the world such as sight, sound, smell, touch, and taste. Everything in the physical realm is processed through your mind. Your mind is open to all thoughts today, both evil and good. You have the ability and freedom to either select or reject thoughts. The thoughts you select are passed onto the heart of man, trying to convince the soul to give the body and mind what it wants.

You have a piece of my Father in you, **the spirit of man.** The purpose of your spirit is to receive communication from My Father's Spirit. When your spirit hears from My Father's Holy Spirit, your spirit works with your conscience to communicate what My Father's Spirit is saying to your spirit. Your spirit speaks directly to your soul. The spirit of man—is confined in the body of flesh we created for you. When I say "of man," I am referring to both created genders, the male and female human being.

We created you **with a soul,** the real you, also known as the heart of man. No human can see your soul because it is confined inside your body. Your soul is eternal—the real you that will live forever.

Today, the instant the physical body dies, your soul and spirit are no longer confined to your dead body. They leave the moment the last breath is breathed out.

The soul is the referee or the decision-making part of all humans.

Your soul receives communication from the spirit of man and your **conscience.** It also receives communication from your body through your mind. Once your soul receives the information, then it makes the decision whether to do what your body is telling it or to do what your spirit is telling it. This process of making choices and decisions is your **free will.**

To summarize how you function: Your body and mind work together, gathering and feeding your soul the wisdom and knowledge of your mind, and the desires and pleasures that your body of flesh senses from the natural surroundings of our creation.

Your spirt functions with the Holy Spirit of God, hearing the direction and will of My Father God. Your spirit communicates directly to your conscience, which, in turn, directs the soul as to what God's messages or will is for you.

Your soul, after receiving information from the body and mind and from the conscience of your spirit, now makes a decision to side with the flesh or with the spirit!

Adam and Eve were created holy, righteous, and pure. They did not have the ability to think any unclean or evil thoughts whatsoever, because My Father is good and not capable of creating evil.

Journalist:

Why did you create humans with a free will? It seems like you set us up to fail. Is that true?

Jesus:

Excellent question. Without **a free will,** your relationship with my Father and me would be robotic. We couldn't have a righteous and loving family relationship with you unless we allowed humans the ability to choose and love. **Love requires you to choose.**

Without love and the ability to make choices freely, you would be like robots, performing my Father's will with hollow and meaningless obedience, because it was not a choice you made from your heart.

Free will allows you the independence to say and do whatever you choose to do. Even if you choose to disobey my Father's principles of creation and His will for humanity, we must honor the choices you make with your free will. Because that is how my Father structured the guidelines of our creation. My Father and I cannot go against **Our Word.**

Journalist:
What was God's purpose in creating human beings?

Jesus:
Our intention for humanity was to have a loving, righteous, and holy relationship with all humans, as Children of God.

We gave you our guidelines for marriage, which is one man and one woman joining together to become one. My Father and I created you with the right to reproduce spiritual beings. We did this because we wanted a family of righteous sons and daughters.

Journalist:
What was life like with Adam and Eve in the Garden of Eden?

Jesus:
Life was really good in the Garden of Eden as my Father and I walked and talked with Adam and Eve in the cool of the day. The bond was holy and righteous as God's Holy Spirit resided in Adam and Eve.

Adam and Eve always chose to please us by being obedient and following the instructions of my Father. Adam and Eve were pure, knowing only my Father's goodness. No evil was in them; only good thoughts existed in Adam and Eve's minds.

The knowledge of good and evil had not been released upon the Earth yet, so, the pleasures and desires of the flesh and body of man didn't control your minds **like it does today.**

It was a magnificent relationship as my Father communed with them. It was exactly what my father intended when we created you.

Journalist:

Jesus, earlier in our conversation, you stated your Father gave Adam and Eve authority and dominion to reign over planet Earth. What did you mean? What authority do we have?

Jesus:

Initially, our purpose for creating humanity was clear. We gave Adam and Eve dominion and authority over the entire earth and all creation. It is written, *"The highest heavens belong to the LORD, but the earth he has given to man."* (Psalms 115:16 NIV)

My Father didn't give ownership of the Earth to you; we assigned the responsibility of governing it to you. Adam and Eve represented my Father and me here on Earth. They were our governors here on Earth.

CHAPTER 4

THE FALL OF HUMANITY

Journalist:

Today, everywhere we see sicknesses, diseases, suffering, starvation, death, and wars. What happened to the good God created? What caused this change? Did God allow this to happen?

Jesus:

This is an excellent question—one that many people have asked me about in many different ways—so let me answer this by going back to the Garden of Eden.

We created humans with a free will, knowing that, when our instructions for creation were disobeyed an evil and rebellious sinful nature would enter into humanity.

In the middle of the Garden of Eden, we put the *Tree of Knowledge of Good and Evil,* among all the other fruit trees, including the *Tree of Life.*

My Father gave Adam one restriction. Of all the hundreds of fruit trees we created for you on Earth, we instructed Adam not to eat from the **Tree of Knowledge of Good and Evil.** Because when he ate of it, he would surely die. My Father put Adam into the Garden of Eden to tend it and keep it. When my Father gave this command to Adam, we had not yet created Woman, Eve.

As I told you earlier, we did not physically restrain or prevent Adam and Eve from eating from the forbidden fruit. Adam, Eve, and you are given the freedom to choose without being forced.

We wanted Adam and Eve to obey our laws of creation out of love and trust. That's why we instructed Adam not to eat from the **Tree of Knowledge of Good and Evil.**

Satan entered the Garden of Eden in the guise of a serpent, which was the craftiest of all the animals my Father and I created. Satan convinced Eve to believe that the forbidden fruit was good to eat and would make her like God—something Satan had already tried to accomplish when he was in heaven.

Eve liked the way the fruit looked. It was pleasing to her. She believed Satan's lie—that my Father and I were strict, stingy, and selfish for not wanting to share our knowledge of good and evil with her and Adam. Instead of remembering the goodness that my Father and I had given her and Adam, she focused on what my father had forbidden.

Eve believed what Satan told her: If you eat from this tree, **"You will not surely die,** for God knows that when you eat of it, your eyes will be opened, and **you will be like God,** knowing good and evil."

Once Eve believed Satan's lie, she took the forbidden fruit and ate it. Then she took some to Adam and convinced him to eat it. The moment Adam ate the forbidden fruit, sin entered the human race.

Journalist:

Did you and God know Adam and Eve would eat this forbidden fruit when you gave them the command not to?

Jesus:

Yes, my Father knows all things; we knew and understood that Adam and Eve would disobey my Father's commands. We also knew sin and unrighteousness would enter the world through them, because

Satan and his evil forces of fallen angels were on the Earth, and that is exactly what happened.

Satan convinced Eve to join him in his rebellion against us by telling Eve, "God is trying to keep something good from you"—implying that my Father God was a liar—and "God knows that in the day you eat from it, your eyes will be opened, and you will be like God, knowing good and evil."

When Adam and Eve disobeyed our instructions, it was a disastrous downfall for the human race. They gained their knowledge of good and evil through the direct experience of believing Satan's lies, instead of receiving the knowledge and wisdom from my Father and me.

It ruined your innocent relationship with my Father and me. It put the entire human race in a disastrous situation. We created you for the purpose of having a righteous relationship. Now, the very purpose of your meaningfulness to my Father and me was shattered, all because of not obeying our instructions of creation. Sin entered the human race through one man.

Journalist:

What did God mean when He told Adam that, when he ate it, he would surely die? They did not die immediately.

Jesus:

When My Father gave that command to Adam, He was not referring to a physical death. He was talking about His Holy Spirit that resided in Adam and Eve being removed from them, causing then to die a **spiritual death** while they were **alive on earth.**

When Adam and Eve sinned, my Father's Spirit was removed from them, leaving a void in their human body, which was replaced immediately by Satan's rebellious sinful nature.

The human race was now under the control of the Evil One, and you became enemies of my Father and me.

Journalist:

Jesus, when you planted the Tree of Knowledge of Good and Evil in the Garden of Eden, didn't that set up Adam and Eve to fail?

Jesus:

Many unbelievers, doubters, and skeptics often complain that my Father and I set up Adam and Eve to fail by giving them a test that was either too difficult or deceptive.

However, we had to give Adam and Eve a choice. Without free will to choose, Adam and Eve would have been mere puppets. **True love** always requires choice.

My Father wanted Adam and Eve to choose **to love** and **trust us.** The only way we could give them choice is to command something that was not allowed.

We planted hundreds of different kinds of fruit trees in the Garden of Eden so Adam and Eve would have a wide variety of fruit to eat.

Of all the fruit in the Garden, only one fruit was forbidden for them to eat. The fruit from the **Tree of Knowledge of Good and Evil** was off limits to them. My Father and I instructed them not to eat its fruit, because, when they ate the fruit, they would surely die.

By eating the fruit of the trees we approved, they were choosing to believe and trust in my Father.

But when they chose to eat the forbidden fruit, their act of disobedience and rebellion against my Father's commands showed us that they no longer believed and trusted my Father and me.

Instead, Adam and Eve believed Satan's instructions. They put their faith and belief in what Satan had told them. When they did this, they gave Satan spiritual authority and head-ship over them and the human race. Even though we created you, we also gave you the authority and dominion over planet Earth. We must honor what you choose.

The test was not too difficult. Adam and Eve had a large variety of fruits from which to choose to eat.

It was a natural choice for my Father and me to forbid the human race not to eat the fruit from the Tree of Knowledge of Good and Evil, because we knew that, when you ate the fruit, you would experience evil and then become evil. My Father and I cannot exist with evil.

We also knew that, when Adam and Eve disobeyed our instructions regarding the forbidden fruit, evil would produce sicknesses, diseases, suffering, hatred, starvation, wars, and death on the Earth we'd created and given to humanity to manage.

This is not what we intended or desired. This is Satan's stronghold and principalities of evil—which he established. This is all a result of Satan's sinful nature and Adam and Eve's choice to believe Satan's lies. My Father is capable of creating only good!

Eve knew she should not eat from the one tree in the middle of the garden. Instead of trusting and obeying my Father and me, after all we had done for them, **Eve chose** to believe the lies Satan told her, believing that we had lied to her.

When they ate the forbidden fruit, they lost their innocence, and their relationship with my Father and me was broken.

They gained knowledge of good and evil, but it wasn't at all what Satan had originally advertised. Just as Satan had lost all he had in the Kingdom of Heaven, so Adam and Eve lost the Kingdom of God from within them.

Journalist:

Jesus, how did you and God feel, and what did you do when Adam and Eve believed Satan and did what he told them?

Jesus:

I appreciate your question. Only a few people have asked me what we felt when Adam and Eve fell away from us.

Use your imagination, and put yourself in my Father's position as creator of all creation. You are observing creation through my Father's eyes—seeing all that you created, including the human race.

You're monitoring how magnificently creation is staying in its place, performing according to your own will and intentions. Everything you created is good and is operating in perfect, righteous harmony. Your Word holds everything in its place.

Then, one day, you observe the children you love so much—the ones you walk and talk with in daily fellowship, the ones you created and gave authority and dominion over planet Earth to manage for you—as they choose to disobey the instruction you gave them regarding the principles and requirements of creation. You watch them eat the forbidden fruit you specifically instructed them not to eat.

Because you know everything, you're fully aware that, when the sinful nature enters them, sin will manifest itself in their bodies, causing them to desire to please the desires of their bodies and minds, and dismiss the things of my Father.

You also know that sin will bind and enslave the entire human race with addictions, illnesses, diseases, and evil, causing disabilities, destruction, war, and death. You look into the future and see that the evilness of Satan's sinful nature will advance in the hearts of humanity, causing them to become so evil that you will regret the day you created them.

Your wrath builds against Satan and evil. You're sad and full of compassion for your children; however, you cannot step in and stop any of it, because you cannot go against your own principles, standards, and precepts of creation. You gave authority to Adam to govern Earth, and now he has given it away to the Devil.

So that you may realize what my Father and I felt when Adam and Eve believed Satan over us, use your imagination for just a moment, and imagine you're the parent of a 10-year-old son and a 9-year-old daughter whom you have raised from birth and love dearly.

You walked, talked, laughed, and enjoyed life with your two children every day, They are wonderful, loving children, knowing only the goodness of people and the world around them. You have instructed and trained them about all the goodness of life, because that's who and what you are.

You told them never to go with a stranger on foot or get into a vehicle with a stranger, no matter what the stranger said or what the circumstances were, because, if they did, they would die.

One day, you watch from a distance as your two children are walking alongside a road. A strange vehicle slows down and stops beside where your children are walking. Your children stop walking and turn, facing the vehicle. They appear to be listening to someone in the vehicle.

After a few minutes, you see the vehicle's back door open. A moment later, your daughter gets into the back seat. You watch, hoping your son does the right thing and screams out or runs away for help.

After a few moments, your daughter reappears out of the car with food in her hands. She offers your son some of the food. He accepts and begins to eat the food, as they both get into the back seat of the car. The door closes, and the vehicle does a U-turn and speeds away in the opposite direction from you.

All the money you'd spent on them and saved for their college fund is now meaningless. All the goodness you taught them and time you spent with them walking, talking, sharing, and planning their life is shattered.

You were a good parent. Of all the hundreds of things that you gave them to use and do, there was only one thing you instructed them not to do: *Never go with a stranger on foot or in a vehicle, no matter what they say, or do, or promise you.*

Because your children focused their attention on listening to someone else—and believed what they were told—they then chose to do what *they* wanted to do, what their mind and body told them to do, resulting in their disobeying your instructions.

They had no knowledge of the evil that would come to them. Their believing in someone else and their disobeying your instructions cost them their innocence, their separation from you, and their lives.

There was nothing you could have done to stop it. You trained them, you loved them, and you wanted them to love, trust, and obey you. Forcing them or interfering with their decision making so they would love and obey you, was not an option, because that would go against your word, your own beliefs, and against your standards you had given them to live by.

There was only one thing they could not do—*never go with a stranger, no matter what.* They disobeyed you, and it changed what you'd intended for your children, when they were conceived and birthed.

Let me ask you: If you were in our position and you had created the Earth for your children to rule and reign, and now they were under the spiritual control of someone else—a stranger—wouldn't you do all that you could do to get your children back?

I'm sorry for taking so long to answer your question, but it is vitally important for people to know and understand **the truth** about the downfall of humanity. Adam and Eve went from being holy and righteous children of my Father God to becoming children of the Devil, opposed to living life the way my Father and I had created them to live.

Journalist:

Thank you for your clear answer. But your answer leaves us hanging: Where does that leave the human race today? What hope do we have of becoming your children again?

Jesus:

Today, all human beings are born directly from their mother's womb with a rebellious sinful nature within them. You are born as sons and daughters of the Wicked One and are an enemy of my Father and me.

As you mature and grow physically, the knowledge of **evil** also grows within you. The **only hope** the human race has is that, somehow, the sinful nature has to be removed from you, and someone needs to provide a way and a right for humanity to choose to be born anew with my Father's Holy Spirit. Somehow, you must achieve a new life, born once again with my Father's Spirit, like Adam and Eve were prior to their fall from grace.

Journalist:

Are you saying that, because Adam made one bad choice and disobeyed God's commands, the human race lost its inheritance as sons and daughters of God, and a physical death sentence was handed out to us?

Jesus:

Yes, that is correct. We created Adam and Eve to be like us. There was no advocacy or any need for it, because the human race knew no evil—they were righteous and holy like my Father and I created you.

Originally, we created humans with an immortal body; you were not created to die. But when Adam and Eve disobeyed my Father's command and ate the forbidden fruit, a sinful, rebellious nature entered into Adam and Eve. Sin brought **two deaths.**

Because Adam disobeyed our command and ate the forbidden fruit, my Father willed me to tell Adam, "Since you listened to your wife and ate from the tree, whose fruit I commanded you not to eat, *the ground is cursed because of you.* In the sweat of your face you shall eat bread till you return to the ground. For out of it you were taken, *for dust you are, and to dust you shall return.*" A covenant of **physical death** went into effect for the human race when my Father willed me to speak these words to Adam.

More importantly, sin provoked the removal of the Holy Spirit's indwelling. Adam and Eve were perfect and holy human beings, but, when sin and the rebellious nature entered into them, the **Holy Spirit** was removed. Sin and holiness cannot coexist.

This caused a severing of your relationship with us, resulting in <u>spiritual death</u> while you are physically alive, leaving you empty, incomplete, and void inside, without the Holy Spirit.

My Father and I love you so much that we had to remove you quickly from the Garden of Eden, because you had the knowledge of good and evil, and you were in a state of sin. If you reached out and ate from the **Tree of Life,** while still in a state of sin, there would be no means for reconciling you back to us. So we removed you from the Garden of Eden and placed a flaming sword that flashed back and forth to guard the way to the **Tree of Life.**

Sin entered the world through one man when Adam sinned. As a result of Adam's sin, the entire human race falls short of the glory of God, and the wages of sin is death. Adam's sin brought death, and death spread to everyone, for everyone has sinned.

Since the day Adam sinned, every human being conceived from the seed of man and born from the womb of woman is born with a rebellious, sinful nature separated from my Father and me, at birth. You are **spiritually dead,** meaning you are separated from my Father and me, while alive on earth.

Unless you choose to ask me to be master of your life, you will live your life on Earth spiritually separated from my Father God.

If you do not choose to believe in me and your body dies physically, at that moment, the destination of your soul is sealed. Your soul is separated from my Father and me for all of eternity.

Journalist:

What happened to the authority and dominion you gave to Adam and Eve?

Jesus:

The authority and dominion that my Father entrusted to Adam over Earth was so complete and final that, when Adam disobeyed my Father's command not to eat the forbidden fruit, he ended up giving it away to the Devil. This caused the entire human race to fall under the spiritual control and influence of the Wicked One.

Satan used this dominion and authority on me about 2000 years ago, after I had been baptized by John the Baptist and was led by my Father's Holy Spirit into the desert wilderness to fast. Satan tempted **me** with the dominion and authority stolen from Adam.

The devil led me up to a high place and showed me in an instant all the kingdoms of the world. He tempted me by saying, "I will give you all their authority and splendor; it has been given to me, and I can give it to anyone I want to. If you worship me, it will all be yours." I didn't argue with Satan because what he said was true, so I told Him, "The Scriptures say, 'You must worship the Lord your God and serve only him.'

Once Adam disobeyed our structure of creation, my Father's Covenant with humanity was broken.

My Father and I fully understood that humans were not capable of attaining righteousness ever again, no matter how much good they did, because the motives of their hearts were sinful.

We also knew that the bondage of evil and suffering resulting from sin and unrighteousness needed a full and permanent plan for reconciliation. This perfect solution had already been worked out by my Father and me before the foundation of the world.

Now spiritual warfare has broken out on Earth. There is a spiritual war of good and evil going on right now between my Father's army of angels and praying saints and Satan and his host of evil angels.

This war is real, and **it's for the possession** of **your soul.** The battleground is your mind, your will, and your emotions for the purpose of dominating your unredeemed soul.

CHAPTER 5

WHY SPIRITUAL WARFARE?

Journalist:

MANY OF US don't understand spiritual life or spiritual warfare. What do we need to know and do in this spiritual war?

Jesus:

Spiritual life is not understood by even the wisest of humans because you have a body of flesh. However, the spiritual realm is real, unseen, alive, and active, and humans cannot function in the spiritual dimension using the same physical senses that the body uses to perform in the physical realm. Your body's senses are designed to operate in the physical realm and do not have the ability to operate in the spiritual world, unless My Father permits you supernaturally to do so or you are controlled by the devil.

Your physical mind doesn't comprehend the spiritual. You cannot see, hear, and feel with your physical senses in spiritual territory, so many people don't even believe in spiritual life. Many of you believe it's a fabrication of someone's imagination. Yet the spirit world is much more alive and vivid than your physical life.

"Your struggle in life is not against flesh and blood, but against the rulers, against the authorities, against the powers of this dark world, and against the spiritual forces of evil in the heavenly realms.

You must understand that the very air around you is filled with hostile forces of evil angels trying to keep you from having a relationship with me and my Father.

You need to learn all you can about your enemy, the devil, who has spiritual control over you. When you are born, you are sons and daughters of the Wicked One, Satan. He keeps you under his spiritual contract by your believing the lies he feeds you. He portrays himself as your friend and advocate while convincing you that my Father and I created you for our own selfish, controlling desires. He wants you to believe that we want you to strictly obey our commands and that, when you don't obey, we are unforgiving, and we punish you.

Journalist:

What do you mean by, "...are Sons and Daughters of the Devil"? How is he still in control of us today?

Jesus:

You give the Devil power by believing his lies. These lies are like a trap that ensnares you into captivity. Most of you don't even realize you have been deceived, because he masquerades as an angel of light.

When you believe Satan's lies, you have become imprisoned and enslaved in bondage to drugs, alcohol, sexual immorality, pornography, food, sickness, diseases, and many other lustful pleasures of your flesh. This is why I told you, "He was a murderer from the beginning, not holding to the truth, for there is no truth in him. When he lies, he speaks his native language, for he is a liar and the father of lies." (John 8:44 NIV)

One of the most deceptive and powerful weapons that Satan uses against you is pride. It is effective because you love to receive praise. You become proud of your work, prideful of your home, prideful of your children, and prideful of whom you have become. Pride dominates you, and, before long, it blinds you from your need for my Father God. Pride convinces your heart you can do things without **God's help** or intervention. Pride is dangerous, because you become hard-hearted and rebellious against my Father, which will lead to the searing of your conscience against Him.

The moment you are born, you are under the spiritual control and bondage to Satan. You are a sinner at birth and an enemy of my Father and me. As you mature, you do so under the spiritual control and influence of Satan. You are a Prisoner of War in Satan's kingdom of darkness.

We knew that the bondage of evil and suffering resulting from sin and unrighteousness needed a full and permanent **plan for reconciliation.** This perfect solution had already been worked out by us before the foundation of the world. You are all prisoners of sin.

However, we loved you so much that My Father paid a ransom to save you from the empty life you inherited from your ancestors. The ransom he paid was not mere gold or silver. It was my own precious blood. God sent me to become your ransom long before the world began, but he has now revealed me to you in these last days. I became the sinless, spotless Lamb of God. You may receive my Father's promise of freedom by believing in me, Jesus Christ.

If you don't choose to believe in me and my Father's plan for your salvation, then you remain separated from us. You are dead to my Father God while alive on earth.

Journalist:

Jesus, what was the ransom? What did you do that paid a ransom for us?

Jesus:

My Father sent me **to set you free** from Satan and the bondage and enslavement and addictions of sin he has you bound with. I did this when I was crucified to death on the cross at Calvary. I was buried in a tomb, and, on the third day, I was raised from death to life by my Father's Holy Spirit.

My death, burial, and resurrection defeated death and destroyed the Devil's strongholds, his principalities, and powers of darkness in the spiritual realm.

Journalist:

What hope do we have that we will be reconciled back to God?

Jesus:

When my Father raised me from death to life, I provided the way and the right for humanity to choose to become a Child of God by believing in me and all that I am. Your hope is kept alive because I am alive, in heaven, and, if you believe in me, I will be with you always.

It requires you humbling yourself, turning from your wicked ways, and seeking a relationship with me and my Father. If you do what I have instructed you to do, I will give you the strength to overcome the ways of Satan.

Journalist:

If I become a child of God, am I protected from the Devil at all times, no matter what I may say or do?

Jesus:

Satan and his demonic forces will try to draw you away from us. He is constantly attempting to block and interrupt you from doing my Father's will and will never stop trying to destroy your relationship with us.

I told my disciples 2000 years ago to remain in me and that I would remain in them. If they loved me and obeyed my teachings, I would always be with them. These same words apply to you today.

The sole purpose of Satan and his forces is to maim you, to inflict wounds on you, to discourage you, so that you will lose heart and fall out of fellowship with my Father. Once the relationship breaks down just a little bit, Satan, like a lion, stalks you, and when he finds you weak enough, he tries to separate you from my Father and me. You become like a single prey, detached from your believing brothers and sisters, and your relationship with my Father and me is disconnected.

When you sever your relationship with us, you become fully exposed and vulnerable physically and spiritually to the lion, Satan. "You must remain alert; the devil prowls around like a roaring lion, looking for someone to devour. Resist him by standing firm in the faith." (I Peter 5:8-9 NIV)

Journalist:
Where does that leave humanity today?

Jesus:
The vast majority of human beings today are not concerned about their separation from my Father and me while alive on Earth. Your interest lies in pleasing yourselves on Earth. And many of you believe that, once death occurs, life stops existing. You don't think about life after death, nor are you prepared for it. Many of you don't care. Your interest lies in living a lifestyle that is dedicated to pleasing the sinful desires of your flesh.

Today, the powers of sin are stronger than you are. You have become enslaved to a sinful nature and are in bondage to addictions and to the desires and lust of flesh. That's why I said, "Everyone who sins is a slave to sin." (John 8:34 NLT)

The only hope you have is if your sinful, rebellious nature, with all your sins, is removed. Then, your relationship with my Father God and me could be restored.

CHAPTER 6

SON OF GOD—SON OF MAN

Journalist:

Jesus, how did you come from eternity in heaven to planet Earth?

Jesus:

When the set time had come, my Father sent me, his Son, born of a virgin woman who was under the Law of Moses, to redeem those under the law, so they might receive adoption to sonship.

My Father sent me to be born as a human being. "The mystery which had been hidden for ages and generations has been revealed to His saints. It was my Father's will to make known the riches of the glory of this mystery among the Gentiles: which is me, Christ, in you, the hope of glory." (Colossians 1:26-27)

Hundreds of years before I was born, the prophet Isaiah prophesied to the Children of Israel that a virgin would conceive and give birth to a son, and that the people would call him "Immanuel."

To accomplish this, an angel of God appeared to a young virgin woman named Mary to instruct her of my Father's desire to use her as the mother of a baby boy to be born to her, and she was to call **His name Jesus.**

Once Mary understood how she, a virgin, would be with child by the Holy Spirit of God hovering over her, she consented to the angel of God her willingness to be the mother of Jesus.

The angel told Mary, "You will give birth to a son, and you are to give him the name 'Jesus,' because he will save his people from their sins."

Mary agreed to do my Father's will and become impregnated by the Holy Spirit. But this caused a serious problem for Mary and her fiancé Joseph. They were not yet married, and she was still a virgin when she became pregnant through the power of the Holy Spirit.

Joseph was having a serious problem understanding Mary's pregnancy. He knew he was not the father of the child that Mary was carrying inside her, because he had not had any sexual relationship with Mary. He also knew Mary to be a good woman and did not want to disgrace her publicly. So he decided to break the engagement quietly. As he considered this, an angel of the Lord appeared to him in a dream. "Joseph, son of David," the angel said, "do not be afraid to take Mary as your wife. For the child within her was conceived by the Holy Spirit.

And she will have a son, and you are to name him 'Jesus,' for he will save his people from their sins."

When Joseph woke up, he did as the angel of the Lord commanded and took Mary as his wife. But he did not have sexual relations with her until I was born. And Joseph **named me 'Jesus.'** (Matthew 1:19-25 NLT)

My Father caused the very first Roman Emperor, Caesar Augustus, which means "exalted one," to order a decree for the entire world to register to pay taxes. Following Jewish custom, the registration took place at the person's ancestral home. I was a direct blood descendant of King David through my mother, Mary, and also by title through Mary's fiancé, Joseph, who later became Mary's husband. I was born in Bethlehem, the city of King David.

The night I was born, my Father made the grandest birth announcement the world had ever seen or heard. That night there were shepherds staying in the fields nearby, guarding their flocks of sheep.

Suddenly, an angel of the Lord appeared among them, and the radiance of the Lord's glory surrounded them. They were terrified, but the angel reassured them, "Don't be afraid!" "I bring you good news that will bring great joy to all people. The Savior—yes, the Messiah, the Lord—has been born today in Bethlehem, the city of David! And you will recognize him by this sign: You will find a baby wrapped snugly in strips of cloth, lying in a manger." Suddenly, the angel was joined by a vast host of others—the armies of heaven—praising God and saying, "Glory to God in highest heaven, and peace on earth to those with whom God is pleased." (Luke 2:8-14 NLT)

When I was eight days old, I was circumcised and named "Jesus." This name was given by the angel before I began to grow inside Mary. (Luke 2:8-21)

Journalist:

When and who helped you begin your ministry as the Messiah?

Jesus:

John the Baptist was the one my Father had selected to prepare the way for me.

In the Prophet Isaiah's day, there were few roads, so when a king or a majestic ruler was coming to visit their area, the people would build roads so that the royal chariot would not have to travel over rough terrain or get stuck in the mud. 700 years before I was born, the Prophet Isaiah said, *"A voice of one calling in the desert: 'Prepare the way for the LORD; make straight in the wilderness a highway for our God.'"* Isaiah 40:3

Prepare means "clear the way." Clear the obstacles away. "Highway" represents the hearts of the people who must be spiritually prepared through repentance for my Father's glory to be revealed on Earth. (Read Luke 3:3-30)

John the Baptist preached out in the wilderness, far away from the temple in Jerusalem. He spoke against the attitudes and rituals of the temple system and the doctrines of society, such as those of the Sadducees and Pharisees. People came by the hundreds to listen to his message. He preached something new, a message of repentance and "change of heart."

The Children of Israel were ready for God to do something new. They were looking and hoping for the Messiah. They were wondering in their hearts if John might possibly be the Christ, the one they were expecting. The Children of Israel expected a Messiah like King David, a leader who would restore Israel's lost glory and even create heaven on Earth. Their wealth would be restored and, once free, they envisioned the Messiah establishing His kingdom, followed by God's judgment upon the world, because of how they had treated Israel.

The authorities from the temple, including the Levite Priests, came to question John the Baptist. They wanted to know who he was. John told them, "*I am not the Christ.*" They asked him, "*Then who are you? Are you Elijah?*" He said, "*I am not.*" They continued to question him, asking, "*Are you the Prophet?*" He answered, "*No.*" Finally they said, "*Who are you? Give us an answer to take back to those who sent us. What do you say about yourself?*" John replied in the words of Isaiah the prophet, "*I am the voice of one calling in the desert,* **'Make straight the way for the Lord.'** (John 1:20-24 NIV)

John told them, "*I baptize you with water. But one who is more powerful than I will come, the straps of whose sandals I am not worthy to untie. He will baptize you with the Holy Spirit and fire.*" (Luke 3:16 NIV)

The reason they kept asking John, "Are you the Christ?" was that the prophets in the Old Testament insisted God would send an "Anointed One," which means "the Messiah" in Hebrew.

A few days later, John the Baptist **spotted me** for the first time. He said, "*Look, the Lamb of God, who takes away the sin of the world! This is the one I meant when I said, 'A man who comes after me has surpassed me because he was before me.' I myself did not know him, but the reason I came baptizing with water was that he might be revealed to Israel.*"

Then John gave this testimony: *"I saw the Spirit come down from heaven as a dove and remain on him. I would not have known him, except that the one who sent me to baptize with water told me, 'the man on whom you see the Spirit come down and remain is he who will baptize with the Holy Spirit.' I have seen and I testify that this is the* **Son of God.***"* (John 1:29-34 NIV)

Immediately after John baptized me, I was led by the Holy Spirit out into the wilderness, where the devil tempted me. He offered me the authority that Adam had surrendered to Him when Adam disobeyed us and ate the forbidden fruit.

Shortly after John the Baptist had been put in prison, I began my ministry. I went into Galilee proclaiming the **Good News.**

John the Baptist was a great prophet who phased out the Old Testament and prepared the way for me to usher in the kingdom of heaven to the Children of Israel, first, and then to all peoples of all nations.

Through me, my Father God is now working out His amazing and mysterious plan of salvation for humanity, which is the greatest story ever told.

CHAPTER 7

JESUS OF NAZARETH

Journalist:

J ESUS, ONE DAY when you were teaching a crowd, you told them that nobody had been born that is greater than John the Baptist; *"yet whoever is least in the kingdom of heaven is greater than he."* Please explain how one of us can be greater than John the Baptist.

Jesus:

Thank you. That's a question that many of my followers need to know the answer to. This is how it took place:

When John was put into prison, he heard about all the miracles, signs, and good deeds I had been doing. But, I had not established Israel as a new kingdom, nor had I set up any judgment. So, John the Baptist sent some of his disciples to ask me, *"Are you the one that is to come, or should we expect someone else"*?

I told John's disciples, "Go back and report to John what you hear and see: the blind receive sight, the lame walk, those who have leprosy are cleansed, the deaf hear, the dead are raised, and the good news is proclaimed to the poor."

After John's disciples left, I told the multitudes there, among all the people born of women, there has not been anyone greater than John the Baptist; **yet whoever is least in the kingdom of heaven is greater than he** (Matthew 11). The "least in the kingdom" refers to those who **will be** in the kingdom that I was ushering in at that time.

Today, if you believe in me and obey my teachings, you are greater than John the Baptist!

Journalist:

Jesus, sorry to interrupt, but how can one of us be greater than John the Baptist?

Jesus:

At the time I said this, I had not been crucified and raised from the dead, and you did not have our Holy Spirit available to you.

Once I came out of the grave, alive, and ascended into heaven, my Father's work on earth was completed. Since that day, everything we have accomplished has been done through a human being who believed in me as Jesus "the Messiah." The mystery has been revealed: you now know my Father's whole plan of salvation.

I'm telling you the same thing I told my disciples the night before they crucified me. Today, you know my finished business. You are my friends if you do what I tell you. I do not call you servants that I own anymore. A servant does not know what his owner is doing. I call you "friends," because I have told you everything I have heard from my Father. (John 15:14-15 NLV)

Journalist:

Jesus, earlier in our conversation and just now, you referred to yourself as a "mystery being revealed." What did you mean by that? Who were you a mystery to?

Jesus:

This is the key question in answering, "Who do you say I am?" why I came to Earth, and what I did while I was here on Earth.

My presence on Earth two thousand years ago was a **mystery** to most of my lost sheep, the Children of Israel. I came to my own race of people, the Jews, but they didn't receive me as the **Son of God.**

Some accepted me as the "Messiah," but the vast majority did not. In fact, they ended up rejecting me.

On the other hand, the evil spirits I encountered knew who I was and called me by my Name. But they didn't understand what I was doing on Earth at this time. They were surprised and mystified.

For example, I encountered two demon-possessed men one day when I had crossed a lake and arrived at the other side. The two men came from the tombs to meet me. They were so violent that no one could pass that way. The evil spirits called out to me, "What do you want with us, **Son of God?**" they shouted. *"Have you come here to torture us before the appointed time?"* Some distance from them, a large herd of pigs was feeding. The demons begged me, *"If you drive us out, send us into the herd of pigs."* I told them, "Go!" So they came out and went into the pigs, and the whole herd rushed down the steep bank into the lake and died in the water. (Matthew 8:29-32 and Luke 8:28)

You see, Satan and his angels of darkness know that, after the final judgment, at the end of the world, they will be thrown into the lake of fire that burns with sulfur, as stated in Revelations 20:10. This is why they were shocked to see me. They knew it was not their time for judgement, but they didn't know why I was on Earth. If Satan really knew what I was doing on Earth, he never would have participated in helping to kill me. It truly was **a mystery to Satan** and **the fallen angels**—why I was on earth at that time.

My presence on Earth was also **a mystery** to most of the Children of Israel. They read, understood, and knew very well the prophetic writings of their prophets. 2000 years ago, the most popular teaching and expectation of the majority of Priests, Sadducees, Pharisees, Temple leaders, and Scholars of the scrolls was that, when "the Messiah" would come, he would do the good deeds written about him and then restore Israel, the nation, and its people by establishing his kingdom as the reigning power on Earth, and *then* institute the judgement.

While I was teaching the multitudes about the kingdom of God, the majority of them thought me to be "The Messiah," but they were looking for a king who would redeem, reconcile, and set the nation of Israel and its people free from the Roman bondage of taxes and slavery and establish Israel as a powerful and mighty nation physically. They wished no longer to be poor but desired to be well off and able to live a good life. They wanted to become the head and not the tail. They wanted and expected their families to be safe from the dominion of Rome.

They expected a king like King David, only greater. They knew Jerusalem was the city where the kingdom was to be established. They envisioned that Israel would **rule the world,** and then **the king would set up His judgement.** This is what many of my followers believed back then.

Today, many of my followers still believe the same thing. They believed I died at Calvary so they could have the wealth of the world restored to them and become the head and not the tail. They don't want to be poor any longer, so their reason for believing in me is that they think I will make them wealthy with the riches from the Prince of this world's systems, Satan.

Journalist:

You were born in Bethlehem of Judea, but most people address you as, **"Jesus of Nazareth."** Why?

Jesus:

Many of the Jewish people were confused with my name and place of birth. "Jesus Christ" was not my full name. "Christ" means "The Messiah" and "The Anointed One." Due to this confusion, many of the Jewish leaders of the synagogue did not accept me as the Messiah, because they knew me as **"Jesus of Nazareth,"** the son of Joseph and Mary.

At the time of my ministry, people were often identified by their native area or place of residence. For example, on the day of my crucifixion, the man who carried my cross when I was no longer able to was called Simon of Cyrene, which noted his name and his place of residence.

This distinguishes him from all other Simons and from all other residents of Cyrene not named Simon. In case there was another Simon in Cyrene, they would add the parents' name to further identify an individual. For example Simon of Cyrene, son of Daniel and Michelle.

Although I was born in Bethlehem, Nazareth was the place where I lived until I began my public ministry. That is why I was said to be "of Nazareth," a Nazarene. They knew my father and mother, but they didn't take the time to learn the truth about me. They assumed I'd been born in Nazareth, and they assumed Joseph to be my natural father.

This is why the Jews complained about me when I told them, "I am the bread that came down from heaven." They said, "Is not this Jesus, the son of Joseph, whose father and mother we know? How is it then that He says, 'I have come down from heaven?'" (Matthew 7:41-42)

The synagogue leaders and most of the common folks knew that "the Messiah" would be born in Bethlehem. But they called me "Jesus of Nazareth." They never took the time to learn about me. **I hope you do!**

Journalist:

Today, it's easy for us to look back in history and understand why you were a mystery for the Children of Israel. That being said, what was your real purpose for coming to Earth?

Jesus:

The prophetic, powerful truth of the Bible is that my Father and I solved the problem of sin once and for all through my sacrifice made on the cross at Calvary for the sins of humanity. The promise given to Abraham was all peoples of all nations would be blessed. I am the **Promised Blessing**—the promise that my Father made to Abraham. I redeemed the entire human race.

My Father showed his love for you by sending me, His one and only begotten Son, into the world as an atoning sacrifice to redeem you from your sins. I am the solution for all sin and unrighteousness. My Father did not send me to Earth to condemn the world but to save the world through me. Whoever believes in me is not condemned, but whoever does not believe in me stands condemned already, because they have not believed in the name of Jesus, the **Son of God** and **Son of Man.**

I am your Messiah. I redeemed you from the Curse of the Law, because it was the Law that held you captive in its condemnation. **Only I** could be the substitute ransom for this bondage. This was my Father's Plan of Salvation all along.

Journalist:

Jesus, what do you mean when you say "pay a ransom"? And to whom did you pay the ransom?

Jesus:

Let me answer this question by sharing with you a little about sacrifices. In the Old Testament, under the Old Mosaic Covenant, animal sacrifice was required for the covering of sins. This appeased my Father, but their garments were sin-stained, and the blood of animals couldn't remove the sin. It only covered it up. So, because the sin was not removed from them, my Father's Holy Spirit could not dwell in the bodies of the Children of Israel.

The only way for my Father's Holy Spirit to dwell in them and you, as he did with Adam and Eve in the Garden of Eden prior to their sin, is for sin to be removed from you. The removal of sin required a ransom that would appease my Father's wrath against sin.

The **ransom price** was far greater than any sinful human could ever pay. The requirements of a ransom were: a human being; the first-born male from the womb who was holy, righteous, and perfect, without any sin whatsoever.

The human race needed a perfect human being willing to die in your place, as a substitute for the entire human race, to be the ransom for all the sins of humanity's past, present, and future.

You needed someone to guarantee the removal of all sin and justify you before my Father. "I redeemed you from the curse of the law by becoming a curse for you.

"I redeemed you in order that the promised blessing given to Abraham, 4000 years ago, might come to the Gentiles through me, so that, by faith, you might receive the promise of the Spirit," (Galatians 3:13-14). Abraham's promise was not to make you rich with Earthly possessions, but to re-unite you with the Holy Spirit of my Father, so that, by faith in me, you could become **Children of God** once again like Adam and Eve.

Journalist:

Jesus, you said you "redeemed" us. What does it mean for a human being to be "redeemed"?

Jesus:

Redemption means to buy back or to save from captivity by paying a ransom. When I was born on Earth, one way to buy back a slave was to offer an equivalent or superior slave in exchange. And God chose to buy you back by offering me, His son, in exchange for you.

You were incapable of retrieving what Adam and Eve had lost in the Garden of Eden. No matter what you tried, you had never found true peace, joy, and purpose in your life. So, I willingly gave up my life in heaven to become your scapegoat, taking your death sentence, so you could live in eternity with me and my Father God. I became your family redeemer.

I **redeemed you,** providing the **way** for you to walk in a spiritual relationship directly with my Father. "I am the only way, I am the Truth, and I am the life, for someone to know My Father. No one can come to my Father God, except through me." (John 14:6)

The story of redemption began in Egypt at twilight on a Thursday evening, when Moses and the Israelites killed the sacrificial lamb and smeared the blood on the doorposts of their homes. They did this so that, when the angel of death that my Father sent saw the blood, he would pass over their home. **This was the first Passover.**

That same night, the Children of Israel began their exodus out of Egypt to freedom. My Father told them, "This is a day you are to commemorate; for the generations to come you shall celebrate it as a festival to the Lord—a lasting ordinance." (Exodus 12:14)

The night that Moses had them kill the lambs and put blood on the door frames of their homes—that was the first Passover. About 1500 years later, I was celebrating the Passover meal with my Disciples in Jerusalem, when I took bread, gave thanks and broke it, and gave it to them, saying, "This is my body given for you; do this in remembrance of me." After the supper, I took the cup, saying, "This cup is **the new covenant in my blood,** which is poured out for you." (Luke 22:19-20)

I was now ready to fulfill my Father's will and purpose for sending me to Earth, to pay the ransom price as the sacrificial Lamb of God, to redeem the human race.

CHAPTER 8

CRUCIFIED FOR YOU

Journalist:

ESUS, I'D LIKE to ask you about the last few hours prior to you being killed on a cross.

Will you share with us your thoughts and feelings of the last few hours of your life, beginning with the last supper, the arrest, and multiple beatings you received prior to your being crucified to death?

Jesus:

Yes. I'll begin on the Thursday evening of your calendar. That was a difficult time for me. As we were eating the Passover supper, I took some bread and blessed it. Then I broke it in pieces and gave it to my disciples, saying, "Take this and eat it, for this is my body." Then, I took a cup of wine and gave thanks to God for it and gave it to my disciples and said, "Each of you drink from it, for this is my blood, which confirms the covenant between God and his people. It is poured out as a sacrifice to forgive the sins of many."

After supper, that Passover night, I was arrested and taken away like a lamb from the manger to be prepared for sacrifice.

I was beaten with wooden staffs, punched in the face, slapped, and kicked by the most brutal soldiers on earth. They stripped me and whipped me with a whip that had sharp pieces of metal tips in the ends of the leather tines. It was specifically designed to tear the flesh from my back and weaken me. My blood splattered and poured from the wounds on my back onto the ground. Then they forced a crown of thorns on my head as more blood poured from my head and ran down my face and body onto the ground. The beatings lasted all through the night and into the early morning hours.

My mind reflected back to six days earlier, when I'd entered Jerusalem and how the large crowds spread their cloaks and cut branches from the trees, spreading them on the road for me to enter their city. The huge crowd welcomed me like a king. They cheered and yelled loudly with excitement, "Hosanna to the Son of David!" "Blessed is he who comes in the name of the Lord!" "Hosanna in the highest!" The whole city of Jerusalem was stirred, as people asked, "Who is this?" The crowds answered, "This is Jesus, the prophet from Nazareth in Galilee, the one with mighty miracles."

Now, six days later, as I stood before the Roman Governor Pontius Pilate, I heard the crowd yelling, "**Away with him,** Away with him! **Crucify him!**"

On the very first Passover Day, Moses led the Children of Israel to freedom from the bondage and the harsh treatment of Egypt. The message from God to Pharaoh was "Let my people go."

Now, nearly 1500 years later, on Passover Day, they led me, "The Lamb of God," outside the city walls of Jerusalem to a hill named "Calvary." They nailed both my hands and feet to a wooden cross. My blood flowed from the cross onto the ground. All the horrific sin, sickness, diseases, addictions, and all the bondage of sin that Satan had put on the entire human race was heaved on me. I knew no sin, but all the past, present, and future sins of the entire human race was heaved on me.

My Father's Will for the New Covenant was put into effect when my blood splattered and spilled on the ground, inside and outside the city of Jerusalem, as I died on the cross at Calvary. I came to destroy the works of the Devil, so you could be set free.

Journalist:

Jesus, what do you mean by "You came to destroy the works of the Devil"? What did you accomplish, and how does it benefit humanity?

Jesus:

The human race is under the spiritual control of the Devil. He has you bound in his powers of darkness and enslaved in bondage to addictions of pleasing the pleasures of your body and mind. You needed deliverance, so through the cross of Calvary is where I would destroy Satan's hold over you.

During my ministry on Earth, Satan had tried several times to kill me but was unsuccessful. I always escaped. Now, at Calvary, it was finally happening. Satan was extremely happy. He had achieved his goal. He had me right where he wanted me—nailed to a cross, a breath away from death.

Satan didn't have a clue that my Father had orchestrated this spectacular plan of sending me, his only begotten Son, as a once-and-for-all-time atonement. It was the perfect sacrifice to pay in full the ransom that God had established for all humanity's sin.

The last words I said on the cross before I died were, "It is finished." And, with that, I bowed my head, gave up the spirit, and died.

Journalist:

What did you mean when you said, "It is finished"? Were you referring to your death or that the mission you'd come to do had been accomplished?

Jesus:

When I cried out, **"It is finished."** I said it as loud as I could speak, for all to hear. I was not talking about my death.

I made a declaration that Satan's authority and control of sin, death, and Hades that he'd held over the human race since the Garden of Eden, **was finished.** I was taking it away from him.

As soon as I said, **"It is finished,"** I breathed my final breath and gave up my Spirit. Satan began to realize what was happening. My Father's New Will was taking place right before his eyes, and there was nothing he could do about it.

Satan suddenly realized the humongous mistake he'd made—a mistake he would never recover from. He thought he had successfully planned my death. But then he realized My Father and I had ambushed him. My death resulted in him being condemned. When I arose from death to life, we destroyed his strongholds and works over humanity, voiding out his headship over the human race.

When I gave up my spirit and died, "At that moment, the curtain of the temple was torn in two from top to bottom. The Earth shook, and the rocks split. The tombs broke open, and the bodies of many holy people who had died were raised to life. They came out of the tombs, and, after my resurrection, they went into the holy city and appeared to many people. When the centurion and those who were guarding me saw the earthquake and all that had happened, they were terrified and exclaimed, "Surely he was the Son of God!" (Matthew 27:50–54)

The spiritual battle became so violent that it manifested into the physical world and tore the thick heavy curtain in the Temple, into two pieces. This curtain separated the holy place, where the priest met daily, from the holiest place on Earth, "The Holy of Holies." where the High Priest of Israel entered once a year to present to me and my Father the blood of a pure one-year-old male animal, who had been sacrificed to us, to cover the sins of the nation of Israel. No one could enter the, "Holy of Holies," and remain alive, except the High Priest and he was allowed to enter only once a year. The torn curtain ended the Old Covenant of "The Mosaic Law," making it obsolete. A New and better Covenant was established.

When I sacrificed my life—my blood, my Father, God, accepted my blood as the one-time atoning sacrifice for all the past, present, and future sins, for humanity. My death, burial, and resurrection, changed the role of sacrifice and confession of sin forever and put the **"New Covenant,"** of my blood, into effect.

Animal sacrifices are finished! I became your one-time sacrifice, providing you a way and a right, which allows you to confess your sinful lifestyle before my Father and be washed in my blood, so you may become reconciled to my Father.

You no longer need to confess your sins to any man on Earth. I am your High Priest and the only one that can provide you direct access to my Father, God, to whom you must confess your sins. There is no other way.

Journalist:

What was the reason for breaking the bones in the legs of the thieves who were crucified with you? And why didn't they break the bones in your legs?

Jesus:

The day I was crucified was the first day of Passover, at which time Jewish law required all activity to cease by the end of the day (the twelfth hour, 6:00 PM).

As a result of the whipping and beatings the night before, I died about 3:00 PM, which was sooner than the two criminals who were crucified with me. Shortly after I died, the Roman soldiers broke the legs of the two criminals to ensure that they would die quickly. The reason for breaking the legs was to stop us from using our legs to push ourselves up to breathe. With broken legs, the pain was too severe to push ourselves up, so we would suffocate much sooner.

I was already dead when they came to me, so instead of breaking my legs, one of the Roman soldiers skilled in marksmanship took his spear and pierced my heart to ensure my death. Blood and water flowed out. They needed to have the dead bodies off the crosses and into our graves before the end of the day to abide by Jewish Law.

I was a human being just like you. I shared a humiliating death, so that, by my death, I might destroy him who holds the power of death, the Devil. (Hebrews 2:14)

They took my body off the cross and laid it to rest in a borrowed tomb.

Journalist:

After you died on the cross they put your body in a tomb, but where did your soul go for the three days between your death and your resurrection?

Jesus:

I want to thank you for asking this question, because the answer to your question is one of the main reasons my Father God sent me to Earth.

Let me share just a little history about death and where your human souls go when you die a physical death on Earth.

Prior to my death and resurrection, when a human died, all dead souls went down to Hades. There were two sides in Hades, a side for the righteous called "Abraham's bosom," and, within shouting distance of Abraham's bosom, but separated by a great abyss, is the second location, Hades Common, which is reserved for the wicked.

Hades Common is a place of torment where fire causes anguish to the souls imprisoned in darkness there. It is the land of forgetfulness, where no work is done, no wisdom exists, and where no one praises My Father God.

Hades Common still exists and is located down under the ground of Earth. It is like a city with gates. The souls of the wicked in the Old Testament and the souls of those who have died and did not believe in me and obey my teachings are in Hades right now in pain, hot anguish, torment, and darkness.

However, the righteous no longer are down under the Earth's ground, in Abraham's bosom, they are **with me in Paradise.**

This changed when one of the thieves killed at Calvary with me sincerely asked me to remember him when I came into my kingdom. I told him, *"Today you will be with me in paradise."*

When I died on the cross at Calvary, my body was laid in a tomb. But my soul went to Hades, where I overpowered Satan on his home turf. I destroyed his strongholds, his principalities, and powers of darkness. I took away from the Devil the authority he had stolen from Adam disarming him of the headship over all people **who would believe in me** and make me Lord of their life.

Journalist:

Jesus, you said you went into Hades, but the Bible says when you died on the cross you said, **"Father, into your hands I commit my spirit."** I'm confused; did you go to Father God in heaven, or did you go into Hades?

Jesus:

Good question. I've been waiting to clarify this because some people have misquoted me and my intentions.

2000 years ago, I was like you in every way, fully human. I had a **body**, a **soul**, and a **spirit**. My body was put into Joseph's tomb. When I died on the cross, the instant I breathed out my last breath, I committed my spirit back to my Father, and my soul went into the heart of the Earth for three days. (Matthew 12:40).

Not only did I bear the wrath of God on your behalf, I also endured physical death and spiritual death, the separation of my soul from my body, and the separation from my Father God. My body was in Joseph's tomb, and my soul was three days in Hades, in the heart of the Earth.

Journalist:

A moment ago, you said "Abraham's bosom" used to be in Hades. What happened? Where is it today, and what caused it to move?

Jesus:

After I finished destroying the Devil's works in Hades, I took the keys of death and the grave away from the Devil. I told all the saints the "Good News" of my coming.

Then I removed the locks and opened the gates of Hades, setting the righteous saints of old free. Abraham, Isaac, Jacob, David, John the Baptist, and all the rest of the Old Testament faithful were ransomed from the power that Satan and Hades had over them, holding them prisoners of war. **I set them free.**

When I came out of Hades, I was the first fruit conquering death— coming back to life. I brought with me, up out of Hades, all those I'd set free from Hades' grave of death. I brought them back to life, with me. They went into Jerusalem and testified about me and what had taken place.

I truly destroyed Satan's spiritual contract over the human race. For everyone who believes in me and all that I am, Satan no longer has authority to come near you, unless my Father or you give him permission.

Journalist:

Jesus, I don't recall hearing about anyone being raised from the dead with you.

Jesus:

Right after my resurrection, in the cemetery outside Jerusalem, the graves were opened, and many bodies of the saints which were dead, arose, came out of the graves, went into the holy city, and appeared unto many people. There were hundreds of eyewitnesses. (Matthew 27:52-53 KJV)

I brought the saints whom I'd set free in Hades back with me up out of Hades. These are the ones who went into Jerusalem and testified.

When I came out of Joseph's tomb, alive, I told my disciples and followers I was dead but to look at me and touch me—I am alive, and I will live forever and ever! And I hold **the keys** of **death** and **the grave.**

Journalist:

What do you mean when you said you "hold the keys of death and the grave"? Aren't death and the grave the same?

Jesus:

Death, to my Father, means to be separated from Him. When Adam and Eve sinned, they became separated from my Father. The Holy Spirit cannot live inside anyone with sin in them. It's the same today: Someone who is separated from my Father is **dead** to us, yet they are alive physically.

If you live a life of sin and you physically die with Satan's sinful nature in you, then you will be separated for all of eternity from us. **That is death!**

I came to Earth to provide you a way and a right to change your death—your separation from God, while you're alive on Earth. But you must make this free-will decision while you're alive on Earth. Once your body dies, your spiritual status and destination is unchangeable.

When I died on the cross, my soul left my body and traveled to Hades, just like the old-time saints. I became separated from my Father, but I wasn't abandoned there. My Father raised me and the Old Testament saints from the dead. My soul was reunited with a now-glorified body, and I held two keys.

The first key is to unlock your death and separation from My Father. In my death and resurrection, I provided you the **way,** the **truth,** the **life,** and the **right** to become a Child of my Father.

The first key of death, separation from God, is free for you to use. If you choose to believe in me and obey my teachings, then my Father God has taken my blood and washed the sinful nature and all your sins away from you and cleansed you and restored you to a state of being holy and righteous, and our Holy Spirit comes and dwells in you.

All of my Father's children come to the cross of Calvary and confess any sinful deed or thought the moment it occurs and we forgive any and all people who sin against them, the instant it happens.

This is why there is no need of a judgement in heaven for my Father's Children. The judgment for sin is on Earth for those of you who believe in me and follow my teachings. I will judge your good deeds and works in heaven and reward you, but there is no need to judge you for sin, because you wouldn't be with me with sin in you. The removal of sin already took place for you on Earth when you confessed all sins and were forgiven.

A true child of my Father God has **two deaths.** The **first death** occurs while you are physically alive on Earth. The moment you choose to believe in me and speak out loud, asking me to be the "Lord of your life spiritually, you've just fired the Devil—causing a spiritual death to sin and the sinful nature and the pleasures of this world.

In dying to sin and Satan, you come alive with our Holy Spirit in you. Satan no longer has any authority over you because you have declared yourself to be a Child of God. **This is your first death.**

Your **second death** is when your physical body dies. In an instant, you will be with me and my Father, forever. Children of my Father will not be judged in heaven for sin, because sin cannot enter heaven, and your sin has already been removed from you while you were on Earth.

The Good News is what I did on the cross at Calvary, what I did in Hades, and what my Father's Holy Spirit accomplished in resurrecting me from death to life, reuniting my Spirit with my body. I did all of this to bring great encouragement to you, so you may face death and seek to do so without fear, knowing the Holy Spirit that raised me from death to life, will do the same for you.

CHAPTER 9

I AM, I SAID ... I AM, SAID I

Journalist:

J ESUS, WHEN YOU came out of the grave alive, can you describe your thoughts and what you felt and what you did?

Jesus:

Yes. Using your current calendar, it was early Sunday morning when I stepped out of death's tomb alive and stood before Heaven, Earth, and Hades, as the undisputed victor defeating Satan and sin. I was full of joy knowing that my Father was pleased because the work He had sent me to do was finished. My Father's will was fully put into effect. But I knew I still had to go to my disciples and explain and reinforce my teachings with them.

Journalist:

What did you do those first few hours after you arose from the dead?

Jesus:

Just a few hours after I arose from the dead, I went to see my disciples. Most of them were together behind locked doors, afraid the Jewish leaders might be coming to kill them. I went into the room, without opening the locked door, and said to them, "Peace be with you!" They were shocked and in awe, thinking they had seen a ghost. So, I repeated, "Peace be with you! As My Father sent me, I am now sending you." *Then,* I breathed on them and said, **"Receive the Holy Spirit."** (John 20:19-22)

Journalist:

What was or is so important about receiving the Holy Spirit?

Jesus:

When Adam and Eve sinned, the Holy Spirit, who was indwelling in them, left their body, and all humans became spiritually dead and remained spiritually dead until 2000 years ago. That's when my Father raised me from the dead. My death, burial, and resurrection provided humanity with **a way** and **the right** to become Sons and Daughters of God by being born again with the indwelling of my Father's Holy Spirit, like Adam and Eve had prior to sin.

I completely destroyed Satan's works, principalities, powers, and strongholds over humanity for all peoples of all nations. I removed the spiritual barriers that had existed since Adam and Eve had sinned. Now you are able, through **my name,** to approach my Father, **repent,** be **reconciled, redeemed,** and be **born again** with His Holy Spirit and walk with us like Adam and Eve did before they sinned. So, on resurrection day, when I breathed on my disciples the breath of spiritual life, they received the Holy Spirit once again.

You asked me how important the Holy Spirit is? It's vital. You cannot enter my Father's kingdom without being born of His Spirit.

Journalist:

Jesus, what instructions did you give your disciples concerning your death and resurrection?

Jesus:

My death, burial, and miraculous resurrection from death to life and ascension into heaven alive, completed my Father's perfect plan of salvation for the human race.

I wish you could sense how wonderful it felt to tell my disciples, "All authority in heaven and on Earth has been given to me. Therefore go and make disciples of all nations, baptizing them in the name of the Father and of the Son and of the Holy Spirit. Teach them to obey everything I have commanded you. And surely I am with you always, to the very end of the age." (Matthew 28:18-20)

Earlier in my ministry, I'd told my disciples, "I will give you the keys of the kingdom of heaven; whatever you bind on earth will be bound in heaven, and whatever you loose on earth will be loosed in heaven." (Matthew 16:19).

I wanted them to understand that the reason I used the future tense—"I will"—was because I had not yet destroyed Satan's strongholds at that time.

Now that I have completed my Father's work, anyone who has faith in me would continue to do what I had been doing and will do even greater things than I had done, because I was going to be with my Father.

I gave them the authority to use my name and taught them how important it was for them to build their relationship with my Father.

And, the most important words I told them was, "If you love me, you will obey what I command."

Journalist:

What did you mean, "...to have a relationship with God..."? How do we have a relationship with God?

Jesus:

I came to Earth so that the human race could have **eternal life** with my Father and me. Eternal life is you getting to know the one and only true God and me, whom He sent. (John 17:3)

The only way you can get to know anyone is by spending time, talking, sharing, and learning about the other person—intimate time spent together, developing a relationship.

Having a relationship with my Father and me is done the same way. You must seek to know what pleases my Father and learn about His will by reading the Bible and praying.

I went through all that I went through so that you could establish your relationship with us. You must get to know my Father and me and learn what rights and benefits you have as a Child of God.

Journalist:

Jesus, is God's perfect plan of salvation and the new covenant different or the same?

Jesus:

That's a magnificent question. My Father's new covenant and His perfect plan of salvation are one and the same.

My Father's new covenant and plan of salvation is the blessing that my Father promised to Abraham when He said, "*All peoples and all nations will be blessed through you.*" I fulfilled that promise, and now it's available to you. "My Father redeemed you in order that the blessing given to Abraham might come to the Gentiles through me, so that by faith you might receive the promise of the Holy Spirit." (Galatians 3:14).

Please understand that the defeat of Satan and his works affects only those human beings who love, believe, and obey me as their Savior. If you don't believe in me, you cannot know my Father, and Satan remains your spiritual father.

Journalist:

Why did we need a new covenant? What was wrong with the old covenant?

Jesus:

When my Father's covenant with Adam was broken, sin and the wickedness of man's heart spread throughout the world from the time of Adam, until the Law and the Ten Commandments were given to Moses. But sin was not charged or counted against anyone's account from Adam to Moses, because there was no Law to obey or disobey until God gave the Law to Moses. But everyone died a physical death from the time of Adam to the time of Moses.

Moses was the mediator of the Mosaic Law, known as the **first covenant.** He was the go-between my Father and the Children of Israel. But Moses couldn't remove your sins. The blood from animal sacrifices was used over and over again to cover the sins of the Children of Israel. The Mosaic Law pointed out their sins and their desperate need of a relationship with their Creator. The Law acted as a jail guard to hold humanity in custody until faith in me was revealed.

The Law was like a teacher: It corrected and instructed the Israelites in my Father's ways until I was revealed, at which time the **Law** was no longer needed.

The old covenant brought you to sin but didn't remove the sinful nature from you.

I fulfilled the Law by ushering in the kingdom of heaven and a New Covenant when I shed my blood on the cross as a one-time sacrifice for all peoples of all nations.

My blood will wash away all your sinful nature and all your sins, no matter what you have done. I provided humanity with a right and a way to come to my Father, through me, and choose, with your free will, to become a Child of my Father God, by confessing your sins and asking for forgiveness. Immediately your sinful nature and sins are removed, and our Holy Spirit comes and dwells in you. You spiritually become born once again, like Adam and Eve before sin. At this very moment, you are perfect, holy, and righteous in my Father's eyes, even though you are a baby believer who needs to learn a new lifestyle.

This is why I am the mediator of the new covenant, which is far superior and much better than the old covenant. I died as a ransom to set you free from the sins committed under the first covenant.

By calling this covenant "new," my Father has made the first one obsolete, and what is obsolete and aging will soon disappear. (Hebrews 7:22, and 8:7, and 13, and 9:15)

My Father's new covenant is a **spiritual legal contract;** it is **binding** and **conditional.** The choice you make is done by your own free will. You may choose to accept me and join the forces of heaven, or you may choose to reject me and remain in charge of our own life. My Father God and I will honor your decision.

If you reject our plan of reconciliation, you will spend eternity with Satan in a place called "Hell," which we created for Satan and his followers. This is not what my Father and I want for you, but we must honor your free-will choice!

I hope that you "Enter through the narrow gate. For wide is the gate and broad is the road that leads to destruction, and many enter through it. But small is the gate and narrow the road that leads to life, and only a few find it." (Matthew 7:13-14)

"Not everyone who calls out to me, 'Lord! Lord!' will enter the Kingdom of Heaven. Only those who actually do the will of my Father in heaven will enter. On judgment day, many will say to me, 'Lord! Lord! We prophesied in your name and cast out demons in your name and performed many miracles in your name.' But I will reply, 'I never knew you. Get away from me, you who break God's laws.' (Matthew 7:21-23 NLT)

My Father loves you so much that He sent me to die in your place.

I love you so much; I obeyed my Father's will for me to come from eternity to Earth and save you from spiritual separation from us forever.

God's perfect plan of salvation is available to you. All you need to do is choose to believe in me and love me enough to obey my teachings.

Or, reject me.

It's your free-will choice.

If you think you can sit on the fence and claim neutrality, you can, but that territory belongs to Satan. It's called "being lukewarm," and my Father will have nothing to do with you if you are lukewarm. He'll spit you out of His mouth. (Revelations 3:15-16).

CHAPTER 10

SON OF GOD, OR ALLAH
AND HIS PROPHET

Journalist:

JESUS, WHY ISN'T Christianity expanding in the Middle Eastern Countries and Northern Africa, where the religion of Islam is embedded and spreading?

Jesus:

Almost 3 billion people in these regions of the world have never heard **the name of Jesus** and the "Good News" about me. The reason is two-fold.

First, the illiteracy rate in these areas is extremely high. Throughout history, their means of communication has been and still is story-telling. They gather together in their villages and share stories and events by word of mouth. Books, newspapers, magazines, and electronic devices are nearly nonexistent in these regions.

The second reason is that the evil Islamic Empire controls its masses by keeping them unaware and totally uninformed about me and my Father's love and great plan of salvation for them.

The people in positions of authority control the vast majority of people in these areas by physically forcing them to follow the religion of Islam. In fact, documented history shows that, from the beginning of the sixth century up to and including yesterday, the Islamic religion advanced its evilness by physical war.

The history books tell us that, as they conquered nations for the land and its wealth, they offered the people of the conquered nations a choice to accept the Islamic faith and live as peasants of Islam or be killed.

Today, the religion of Islam is still being advanced by force through hate, deceitful lies, murder, beheading, and outright war. Today, when they confiscate a nation, they offer the same option they have for hundreds of years: Either accept Islam and live, or be killed.

Journalist:

How and when did the Islamic religion begin?

Jesus:

I'm glad you asked that question, because most people don't know the truth about the false doctrine of Islam.

About 300 years after I finished my Father's work here on Earth, between 312 and 313 A. D., the Roman Emperor Constantine the Great signed an agreement which ensured religious tolerance for people who believed in me—the Christians. This agreement granted Christians the freedom to worship, and it brought an end to my followers being murdered, which began right after my death, resurrection, and ascension into heaven.

Christians were given rights, including the return of stolen property that had been taken from them, and they were given the right to organize churches.

In 324 A D., Constantine established his seat of power in the mostly Christian Turkish city of Byzantium, which was renamed Constantinople, and today is Istanbul, Turkey. By 325 A. D., Christianity was declared the world religion by Constantine the Great.

About 250 years after Constantine The Great made Christianity the world religion, Mohammed was born in 570 A. D.—in the city of Mecca, located on the Arabian Peninsula. Mohammed claimed he had a revelation from a god named Allah, instructing him, Mohammed, to be the teacher of a new faith, called Islam, which means, literally, "submission." This new faith incorporated aspects **of Judaism** and **Christianity.**

He also claims that Allah told him he was the final prophet and that, therefore, the revelations he received were God's final words, overruling all of my Father's other declarations, including me and what my Father sent me to accomplish. Mohammed dictated to people to write down his ideas, which he claimed were revelations from his god Allah, into a book called *The Qur'an.*

Mohammed did the same thing Satan had done in the Garden of Eden. Mohammed took my Father's words, twisted them, changed them, and made them come out appealing and beneficial to the people he spoke with. However, what Mohammed claimed and what he dictated in *The Qur'an* is not true.

Mohammed read through the "Torah," the first five books of the Holy Bible written by Moses about 2000 years before Mohammed was even born.

Mohammed copied our holy scriptures and changed them. He identified Abraham as Islam's ancient patriarch, in which Islam could trace its heritage through Abraham's son Ishmael.

To put this into perspective, Abraham's wife Sarah, after several years of marriage, had not given birth to any children for Abraham. She knew my Father had promised Abraham and her many descendants. So she took matters into her own hands and put her Egyptian slave woman, Hagar, into Abraham's bed so that Abraham could sleep with her and she could raise a family for Abraham through her offspring. Abraham agreed.

Hagar became pregnant with a son they named Ismael, born about 2080 B. C. But this was not the son my Father promised Abraham.

My Father will never go against His own will and word. At creation, my Father created woman as a helpmate for man. One woman and one man joined together are the standards by which my Father God has established marriage and children to be born in marriage. Anything else is a standard established by man and/or woman.

About 15 years later, in 2065 B. C., Isaac was born from the womb of Sarah and the seed of Abraham, as intended and promised by my Father. About 15 years later, Abraham took Isaac to the mountain my Father showed him, Moriah, and offered Isaac up as a sacrifice.

Throughout the Holy Bible's first five books, the Torah, Isaac is the only begotten son my Father God, promised to Abraham.

Mohammed actually went back in history 2500 years and changed the Torah's factual documentation of Isaac being the covenant son, my Father had promised to Abraham and Sarah, **to Ishmael** being the promised son of the covenant. Mohammed literally changed the whole story and rewrote history with his twisted, deceiving lies that are believed by billions of people, because they have never heard the Good News about me and my Father's true kingdom of heaven.

Mohammed twisted the Torah and named it *The Qur'an*, which is the foundation of the false religion of Islam. Then, Mohammed set the example for the Islamic religious sects to follow by waging war against non-believers, killing millions over the years who would not submit to his self-made, counterfeit Islamic religion.

This is still a common thread for many Islamic sects today. They call it *Jihad*—"holy war"—against those who oppose them and their beliefs. They take particular joy in beheading Christians.

Satan has built a vast Islamic empire over the past 13 centuries, unrivaled by anyone. Beginning 600 years after I was crucified, arose from death, and ascended into heaven, completing my Father's work on Earth, Satan and his evil forces used a self-proclaimed false prophet named Mohammed to invent the religion of Islam.

Mohammed began by declaring that my Father God—who is the God of Abraham, Isaac, and Jacob—and Allah is the same god.

Mohammed refers to me as a good man and prophet of Allah. But *he* was the *last* prophet, so his revelation supersedes mine and everything that I'd done.

He also said that the previous words of my Father God—for example, the **Torah,** the **Psalms,** and **the Gospels**—had been superseded by Mohammed's dictation of his fabricated *Qur'an.*

Today, nearly one-quarter of the earth's population believe in a false god named Allah, who was developed by a man who was born from the seed of a human father and died. Mohammed claimed to be a prophet of a god, but neither he nor his god Allah had or have any power.

Journalist:

Wait a minute: Aren't the Torah and The Qur'an basically the same?

Jesus:

No! They are not the same. The Torah consists of Genesis, Exodus, Leviticus, Numbers, and Deuteronomy, the first five books of the Holy Bible. The Torah was written by my Prophet Moses and documented in history about 1600 years before I was crucified on the cross at Calvary.

Over 2000 years after Moses wrote the Torah, Mohammed took it and re-wrote it. He twisted, misquoted, added, and deleted parts of my Father's Abrahamic covenant and some of the Old Testament covenant with Moses and established his own self-made Islamic religion of twisted truths, called **Islam.**

Journalist:

I'm a little confused. I have been told that Mohammed was a prophet of the same god that you call your Father. Is that true?

Jesus:

No. Mohammed was not a prophet of my Father's kingdom, which I ushered in when my Father sent me to Earth to complete His will for the human race.

Journalist:

If Mohammed is not from God, what has he done to deserve to have such a large following of people? Where did Mohammed come from? What are his accomplishments?

Jesus:

That is an excellent question. While Mohammed was alive, he never accomplished any miracles, signs, or wonders witnessed by anyone. The Qur'an verifies what I am saying.

Mohammed was born from the seed of a human father and died. He is still dead. His bones are in his tomb, which is visited by millions of people each year. Mohammed never overcame death. Allah couldn't raise or didn't raise Mohammed from the dead, because Allah is a counterfeit god, with no authority or power over life and death.

Neither Allah nor Mohammed can change a person's heart or save a soul from spending eternity in the "Lake of Fire." Only my Father and I can do that.

Journalist:

Jesus, what does God's Covenant with Abraham have to do with Mohammed?

Jesus:

First, let me review with you what is recorded in the Holy Bible. Then I will interject what Mohammed did to change the truth.

My Father spoke to Abraham when Ishmael was 13 years old and told him, "I will bless Sarah and give you a son from her! I will bless her richly, and she will become the mother of many nations. Kings of nations will be among her descendants." Abraham bowed down to the ground, but he laughed to himself in disbelief. "How could I become a father at the age of 100?" he thought. "And how can Sarah have a baby when she is ninety years old?

Abraham asked my Father, "May Ishmael live under your special blessing?" My Father told Abraham, **No**—Sarah, your wife, will give birth to a son for you. You will name him **Isaac,** and I will confirm my covenant with him and his descendants as an everlasting covenant. As for Ishmael, I will bless him also, just as you have asked. I will make him extremely fruitful and multiply his descendants. He will become the father of twelve princes, and I will make him a great nation. But my covenant will be confirmed with Isaac, who will be born to you and Sarah about this time next year." (Genesis 17 NLT)

Isaac was born according to the Spirit, unlike the first son Ishmael, who was born according to Sarah's plan to have her Egyptian servant, Hagar, have children through Abraham so she could have a family. (Galatians *4:28-31* and Genesis Chapters 16 and 17.)

When Isaac was about 16 years old, my Father said to Abraham, "Take your son, your only son, Isaac, whom you love, and go to the land of Moriah, and offer him there as a burnt offering on one of the mountains of which I will tell you." (Genesis 22)

Abraham got up early the next morning and traveled to where my Father God had told him. He built an altar, placed wood on it, and bound his son, Isaac, and laid him on the altar. Abraham offered Isaac up to God as a sacrifice. Abraham then took his knife to slay his son. (Genesis Chapter 22)

The Angel of the Lord spoke to Abraham, saying, "Do not lay your hand on the lad, for now I know that you fear God, since you have not withheld your son, **your only son, from me.** Then Abraham lifted his eyes up, and there behind him was a ram caught in a thicket by its horns. So Abraham offered the ram up as a burnt offering instead of his son.

Then, my Father spoke to Abraham a second time, saying, *"By Myself I have sworn, because you have done this and have not withheld your son, your only son, I will surely bless you and make your descendants as numerous as the stars in the sky and as the sand on the seashore. Your descendants will take possession of the cities of their enemies, and* **through your offspring all nations on earth will be blessed,** *because you have obeyed me."* (Genesis 22:16-18 NKJV)

Because Abraham obeyed my Father's request to sacrifice Isaac, my Father guaranteed the fulfilment of the Covenant he'd made with Abraham and He promised to confirm with Isaac.

Isaac was the only begotten son of his father Abraham, because **Isaac** was the only son that my Father promised Sarah and Abraham. It was their seed, **Isaac,** which my Father would honor His Covenant with, **not Ishmael.**

Journalist:

Jesus, what does this covenant, Abraham, and Isaac have to do with Mohammed and Ishmael?

Jesus:

One of the major changes Mohammed made and wrote in *The Qur'an* was that he replaced **Isaac** with Ishmael as the son of my Father's covenant. Mohammed discarded the true and real promises that my Father promised Abraham. He justified this by claiming that Ishmael had first-son rights (*not Isaac, as the bible says*) and that Ishmael and his descendants were the children that my Father God's covenant was blessed with (*not Isaac and Jacob*, as the Holy Bible says).

Then Mohammed took it a step further by claiming it was Ishmael that Abraham took to be sacrificed, ***not Isaac***, on Mount Moriah.

When Abraham asked my Father, "May Ishmael live under your special blessing?" my Father told Abraham, *"No—Sarah, your wife, will give birth to a son for you. You will name him **Isaac**, and I will confirm my covenant with him and his descendants as an everlasting covenant.*

The story of Abraham and Isaac was a shadow of what was to come. It demonstrated the parallel between the ram offered as a substitute for Isaac on the altar and me offered on the Cross as a substitute for all humanity.

Because Abraham willingly obeyed and gave up his son, **Isaac,** my Father willingly gave me up, to fulfill the promise that He made to Abraham that, "Through Abraham's descendants all peoples on earth will be blessed." (Genesis 12:3, and 18:18 and 22:18)

Journalist:

So, the covenant was for Abraham's descendants through Isaac, correct?

When you speak of the promise God made to Abraham, is the promise something separate and different from the covenant?

Jesus:

Yes, **Isaac** is the promised covenant son my Father promised to Sarah and Abraham. Moses documented this in the Torah about 2500 years before Mohammed was ever born.

But Mohammed re-wrote and changed the 2500 year old Torah and renamed it *the Qur'an*. Mohammed rewrote *the counterfeit Qur'an* to read *"Ishmael and his descendants"* would be the beneficiaries of my Father's covenant with Abraham. Mohammed swapped the **truth** for a *lie*, and millions believed him and his *counterfeit* documentation of *the Qur'an*.

What Mohammed did doesn't change what my Father God said and did 2500 years earlier—that **is and will always be the truth.**

It is vital that you come to know and understand ***the blessing*** of the promise, my Father made to Abraham, which is: All peoples and nations will be blessed through Abraham.

Journalist:

Jesus, what is the blessing of the promise God made to Abraham?

Jesus:

Adam and Eve had the Holy Spirit of God indwelling in their bodies until they sinned. When they sinned, My Father removed His Holy Spirit from them, because sin and God cannot coexist.

I redeemed you so that the blessing given to Abraham might come to the Gentiles through me, so that by faith you might receive the promise of **the Spirit.** (Galatians 3:14).

The blessing God promised to Abraham was the reuniting of the **Holy Spirit** and humanity once again. If you believe in me and have made me Lord of your life, then you are Abraham's seed and heirs **according to the promise.** (Galatians 3:26-29).

The answer to your question, "What is the blessing of the promise?" The blessing is that, by faith, you might receive the promise of the Spirit, by believing in me.

Journalist:

Was Abraham's promise a secret?

Jesus:

I would describe the promise as a 2000-year-old mystery that had been kept hidden for ages and generations, but my Father chose to make known among the Gentiles the glorious riches of this mystery, **which is me being in you, the hope of glory.** (Colossians 1:26-27).

Journalist:

Jesus, the Arabic word for God is "Allah." Isn't it possible that the Arabic-speaking Muslims believe and pray to the same God that you say is your Father?

Jesus:

If the Arabic-speaking people believe that the name for my Father in their language is pronounced "Allah," I welcome their recognition that my Father God is the God of Abraham, Isaac, and Jacob, and that the descendants of Isaac are the ones who fall under the Abrahamic Covenant and the Mosaic Covenant, given to Moses by my Father.

However, if the Arabic-speaking people are recognizing Allah as a separate and different God from my Father, who is the only true God, then Allah is a fictitious god, with no power or authority to defeat death, perform miracles, or save them by providing a way to Heaven. And I assure you that *Mohammed had no knowledge or wisdom of how to get into the kingdom of heaven.*

Please understand that the fictitious god that Mohammed created named "Allah" and My Father are not the same god. I came to Earth to do my Father's will and to testify on His behalf that He is the only true and Most High God. **There is no other God.**

Mohammed was not a prophet of my Father God and the Kingdom of Heaven. *Mohammed is a **false prophet**, operating as an agent of Satan,* who has established his own teachings mixed with some of my Father's structure and precepts of creation and covenants of the Old Testament and the twisted lies he made up about Abraham.

It's time my Disciples expose the **religion of Islam** for what it really is. My Father's glory will be with them.

The people in these regions need to know the truth about my Father God's covenant with Abraham and about the promise my Father made to Abraham. They need to know we love them and want them to establish a relationship with us. If they do, we will come and live in them. Please tell them we love them.

Journalist:

Jesus, in summary of your comments of Mohammed and what he wrote and did, are you saying that Mohammed actually tried to replace you with himself, making him God's last messenger?

And he replaced your Father, God—with Allah, by saying they are one and the same god? Have I described your explanations correctly?

Jesus:

May I elaborate a little on your statement and questions?

Journalist:

Yes—feel free to.

Jesus:

Satan and his forces want you to compare me, the only Begotten Son of the only true and Most High God, to another human man who was born from the seed of human being and is **an enemy** of my Father and me and everything that we represent.

How can you compare my resurrection to the bones and remains in the tombs of Mohammed and/or Buddha? And what miracles has Allah done?

My death, my burial in death's tomb, guarded by the world's best soldiers, and my resurrection from death to life never to die again was witnessed by at least 513 people and documented by these eyewitnesses.

I ascended into heaven alive, never to die again. This is why I am the Savior of the entire World. Whoever believes in me and all that I am shall spend eternity in Heaven.

Whoever does not believe in me will spend eternity in the Lake of Fire with their father, the Devil.

The documentation of my death, burial, and resurrection began immediately after I ascended into heaven alive and continued for about 60 years by eyewitnesses.

Stop, for just a moment, and reason with me: Imagine that you're a juror, sitting in a courtroom, listening with your own ears, as 513 eyewitnesses testify that they saw me alive, eating, speaking, and walking, and all of them confirm that this occurred during a time frame of 45 days after my death, burial, and resurrection.

Let's say that that each one of the eyewitnesses testifies for 10 minutes on the witness stand under oath. That's a total of 85 1/2 hours of testimony from more than 500 people who saw me alive after I was buried in a tomb.

If you're a juror and you listen to 513 eyewitnesses testify for more than 85 hours that they saw me, Jesus of Nazareth, alive and well, are you going to believe them, or are you going to choose to ignore their testimony and believe Mohammed's writings about how to get to heaven? His writings are bogus. Mohammed's soul is not here in Paradise with me.

No matter what your nationality, race, or culture, **I am your Savior.** I love you, and I will forgive you no matter what you have done, if you humble yourself and repent from your heart of your sins. I am the way and the truth and the life. No one comes to the Father except through me.

You are prisoners of war in Satan's kingdom of darkness, and **only I can set you free.** My Name is Jesus, and I am the Savior of the World. Salvation is found in no one else, for there is no other name under heaven given to men by whom you must be saved.

CHAPTER 11

STARTING LIFE OVER, IT'S YOUR CHOICE

Journalist:

JESUS, I HAVE been around churches where rituals, memorized prayers, and routine programs are followed, but what you have described is a bit rebellious toward the organized religions that I am familiar with.

Is what you're describing a new religion or a way of life?

Jesus:

Yes, it is a refreshing new way for you to choose to live; however, it's not new. My Father and I created this life for Adam and Eve. It's what we intended for all humanity. Adam had it and lost it. Becoming one of my disciples and following my teachings is not a religion.

Journalist:

So, since the downfall of the human race and the removal of the Holy Spirit from our bodies, you and Father God have done what you have described to us today, for us. **Why?**

Why would God do all that you have said He did for us?

Jesus:

Because **we love you!** Human beings are our greatest creation. You are the apple of my Father's eye and the reason for creation.

My Father loves the human race so much that he sent me, his only begotten Son, so that whoever believes in me, should not perish with the Devil in the lake of fire, but have everlasting life with me and my Father. I died for you, so you could exchange your old lifestyle for a new life full of my goodness.

Journalist:

What do we need to do exchange our old lifestyle we live today for the new life you have told us about?

Jesus:

You must believe that what I have told you about my Father is true and establish a loving and obedient relationship with us, by doing His Will.

Your belief, on Earth, will determine your destination for eternity.

Believing is a verb. Verbs require action and behavior. If you believe in your heart in all that **I am,** then you will **love** and **obey** what I commanded you to do. "If you keep my commands, you will remain in my love, just as I have kept my Father's commands and remain in his love." (John 15:10 NIV)

Believing produces action and behavior. Your behavior on Earth will determine your rewards in heaven or your restitution in hell.

Believing in me includes loving and obeying my teachings. The Bible does not separate me from my teachings. "Whoever has my commands and keeps them is the one who loves me. The one who loves me will be loved by my Father, and I too will love them and show myself to them." (John 14:21)

"Anyone who loves me will obey my teaching. My Father will love them, and we will come to them and make our home with them.

Anyone who does not love me will not obey my teaching. These words I am saying to you are not my own; they belong to my Father who sent me." (John 14:24)

If you do not believe in me and or do not obey my teachings, you will spend eternity in "the lake of fire" with Satan and his demons. You will die in your sins unless you believe that I am who I claim to be.

Do you want real peace, real joy, and real purpose in your life? Do you want freedom from the bondage and addictions of sin —alcohol, drug addiction, pornography, or an angry, unforgiving nature? Whatever Satan has you a slave to, **I will set you free** from—the burden and bondage of sin.

Journalist:

Jesus, did you really mean no matter what a human being has done, God will forgive them? What about someone who is a drug dealer, or murderer, or prostitute, or what if someone has been saved before but is not obeying your teachings and is living a lifestyle of sin?

Jesus:

Yes, no matter what: If anyone wants to meet me right now, please allow me to introduce myself to you. My name is **Jesus,** Son of Man and Son of the only true, most High God. I am God's only begotten Son. I love you, and, no matter what you've done, I will forgive you. I will forgive you all your sins, your shame, your guilt, your sorrow—anything and everything. Nothing will remain to condemn you.

The reason I died for you was to satisfy my Father's wrath against sin and to void Satan's spiritual control, which keeps you in a sinful state. When I set you free, you will be free, indeed.

Maybe you thought you were saved, and now you're not sure. Or maybe you ran away from my Father God, or maybe you've never had a relationship with my Father and me.

All you need to do is to **humble** yourself, **turn** your back on your old sinful and selfish lifestyle, and, **from your heart,** ask me to wash and cleanse you of your sinful past. As long as you mean it from your heart, I will **immediately** forgive you from all sin, shame, guilt, and sorrow.

If you confess with your mouth that I, Jesus, am Lord, and **believe in your heart** that God raised me from the dead, you will be saved. For it is with your heart that you believe and are justified, and it is with your mouth that you confess and are saved.

As the Scripture says, anyone who trusts in me will never be put to shame, for there is no difference between Jew and Gentile. I am the same Lord, and my Father is the same God of all; He richly blesses all who call on me. "Everyone who calls on the name of the Lord will be saved." (Romans 10:9–13)

Once you have done this, sin and the sinful nature are totally and immediately removed from you. *Then,* my Father's Holy Spirit will immediately come and live in your body, just like He did in the Garden of Eden, with Adam and Eve.

When you pray the prayer above and mean it from your heart, my Spirit comes and dwells within you. **You start life all over again,** burden free, with me abiding in you.

I conquered death for you. I voided Satan's spiritual power over you, providing you **the right** to become Children of God. It's for all who choose to believe and accept me as Lord of their life.

No other man or god has overcome death. No other man or god has prepared **a way** and **a right** for you to have your soul cleansed of your sinful nature and have a direct relationship with My Father and me.

No other human being is needed—no more priests, no more rituals, and no more memorized or printed prayers with a saint's name on it. All you can and need to do to begin to start life over and begin a **New Life** with me and my Father is to believe from your heart what I have just shared with you.

Just love us from your heart, mean it, and lay down your old life, exchanging it for the new one, making me Lord of your life, so that my Father's promises and will may be done in and through you.

There is nothing else you can or need to do to earn your salvation.

I am not a religion. I am the Savior of the world. No matter what you have done I will forgive you. No one can come to my Father God, except through me. Soon I will come and bring my salvation to those who believe in **me.** My Rewards are with me.

Journalist:

Jesus, I want to thank you for your time and sharing with us. May I ask you just a few more questioners concerning life after death?

Jesus:

Yes, I am always available to you or anyone who is seeking to know about me or my Father.

CHAPTER 12

AFTER WE DIE, THEN WHAT?

Journalist:

What if today is my last day on Earth? Life as I know it is over. I breathe my last breath, and, in the blink of an eye, I'm gone off into eternity. **Then what?**

What is going to happen to me when I die?

Jesus:

What a remarkable question. I say that, because, in today's, world, most human beings act and believe that the most important thing on Earth is living, and, once death comes, life stops, and it's the end—there is nothing more.

Very few human beings think about life after death in the spiritual realm. Most of you are not prepared for life after death, and many of you don't even care.

Physical death is the reward for your sins on Earth, and every single sin is connected and leads to physical death. Sin entered the world through one man, and death through sin, and, in this way, death comes to all people, because all have sinned.

When death occurs in you, your soul leaves your body for another location in eternity.

The spirit of man is set free to travel back to my Father, from where it came.

Your body then becomes a corpse, an empty shell. The physical body's usefulness has been served, and you return to the dust of the ground, from which it came.

Physical death does not affect the soul of man. The soul, **the real you,** lives forever in eternity somewhere.

When you see the lifeless body lying in the casket, many of you believe Satan's lie that the end has come and that life is over. This is why **most people fear death.** You try to run from death, because you think it's final: life ends, and it's over.

Satan wants you to live your life on Earth in fear of death, but I have conquered death, and, while you are alive on Earth, my Father is offering you a gift of eternal life—if you believe in me as your savior. However, if you do not believe in me while you are on Earth, **there is no second chance.**

The truth is that physical death is not the end. The length of your life on Earth is like the vapor of a match. When you light it—*poof!*—You're vaporized off into eternity!

Journalist:

Jesus, will you tell us what we can expect life to be like in eternity?

Jesus:

The first thing that will happen when you die is that your soul will leave your body, and you'll be faced with the realization that my Father God and I really exist and that everything I have told you is the **Truth.**

Your soul will travel into eternity to Paradise to be with me.

If you have not believed in me and accepted me as your savior, your soul will travel to Hades, to await the judgment. Suddenly you understand that the opportunity to choose your destination for eternity is sealed. No situation or condition can alter your destination.

You'll realize that **Heaven is for real** and that believing in me, Jesus, was the only way in.

Or, you'll realize **Hell is for real.** Your belief in the compromising doctrines of religion has landed you in a location that is full of demons of all shapes and sizes and the darkest darkness you will ever witness. And now, it's too late to ask for forgiveness.

How will you feel when you realize Mohammed, Lord Buddha, the Hindu gods, and all the other mystic gods people have invented, are with you in Hades? And some of them are giant demons.

Journalist:

Jesus, I have two questions in one.

One: You mentioned judgment for those who went to Hades and not the ones that went to be with you in Paradise. Aren't both Christians and non-believers going to be judged?

My second question is:

Will God judge us all?

Jesus:

I'll answer the second question first. "My Father, God, has given me the authority to judge every human being because I am the Son of man." (John 5:27-29)

"Each person is destined to die once and after that comes judgment." (Hebrews 9:27).

Now I will answer the first question: Aren't both Christians and non-believers going to be judged?

Let me answer with a soft "Yes." There will be two separate and two different judgments at two different times.

The first judgment is actually a rewards ceremony. It's where I will judge the **works** and **deeds** of my Saints and believers in me who did my Father's will. These are the ones the Bible refers to as **the living** and **the righteous.** (II Timothy 4:1) Also read John 5:22-30.

The timing for the judgment of deeds and works and rewards ceremony will take place right after my appearing when I rapture all my saints and **righteous** believers—both those who have died and are in the grave and the living ones on Earth—and gathered them to me in heaven. Then, I will judge the good works and deeds of my Saints and reward those whose works and deeds have meet the criteria and passed the test.

There is no need to judge my Saints and believers who did my Father's will. They have already confessed and been cleansed of all their sins while they were alive on earth. (They confessed their sins daily to my Father.)

The **second judgment** will take place at another time and place. At this judgment, I will judge every human being who did not believe in me. They are referred to as the unbelievers or the unrighteous—**the dead.**

I will judge Satan worshipers, the followers of Mohammed and Allah, those who believe in the Hindu gods, Lord Buddha's followers, and all others.

I will judge all who claimed to be my followers but obeyed only some of my teachings and disregarded my teachings that they did not like. This includes lukewarm unbelievers. Where, when, and how I judge them may surprise many of you.

There are two separate judgments.

One of **the living.**

One for **the dead.**

CHAPTER 13

REWARDS FOR THE BELIEVERS

Journalist:

Y OU SAID PEOPLE will be raised from the dead. What kind of body will we have? Will it be a physical or spiritual body?

Jesus:

When I come to rapture my Church, the believers who have already died will be raised first, and then my believers who are alive and remain on Earth will be caught up to meet us in the air. The body my believers will be raised up to meet me with is an immortal body.

Your physically aging and decaying bodies of flesh and blood cannot enter my Father's eternal Kingdom. It doesn't matter whether the physical bodies of my Disciples are in a grave or alive when I come to get my Church. Your mortal body will be transformed into an immortal body in the blink of an eye. (I Corinthians 15:51-53)

Journalist:

At the judgment of the believers, what is it that you will be judging?

Jesus:

Once I have raptured all the righteous believers, all the believers must appear before my judgment seat so that each one may receive what is due him for the things done while in the body, whether good or bad. (II Corinthians 5:10)

Your works will be tested. What you did with your life as a believer is tested. It will endure like gold, silver, and precious stones in a fire. Or it will burn up like straw. Not a trace will remain, no matter how sensible, enjoyable, or even religious your activities might have seemed while you were alive.

I will reward you for all your good works and deeds performed for things done in the body.

Journalist:

What criteria will you use to judge the saints' deeds and works?

Jesus:

When you stand before me at your rewards ceremony, I will use three standards to determine if the works you do will endure my test:

1. Your relationship is the first criterion:

The first criterion used to determine your rewards in heaven is your relationship with me and my Father God. "Whoever has my commands and obeys them, he is the one who loves me. He who loves me will be loved by my Father, and I too will love him and show myself to him."

"Anyone who loves me will obey my teaching. My Father will love them, and we will come to them and make our home with them." (John 14:21 and 23 NIV)

Your relationship with my Father must be that of a son and Father. The question I will ask is: Did you establish a loving and obedient relationship with me and my Father?

My Father must be first in your life. If you try to limit your time of reading and praying with God and attempt to balance other interests, such as job, money, and family, then you are using my Father. You are trying to have an affair with Him, and He is not into affairs.

My Father wants a relationship where He is first in your life. Seek first the kingdom of my Father God and His righteousness, and then other things will be added unto you.

2. The motive for doing the good works and deeds is the second criterion I will use:

What was in your heart when you did good deeds? What was your purpose in doing the good deeds? I told you, "Be careful not to practice your righteousness in front of others to be seen by them. If you do, you will have no reward from my Father in heaven." (Matthew 6:1)

The motives of the heart are the key to the reason you performed the deeds. Your motive should be to serve my Father and bring Him glory. Even ordinary actions like eating and drinking can bring God glory. Your most religious actions are worthless if your motive is to build up your ego and reputation. Your motive must be to bring glory to my Father, God.

3. The third criterion is Love:

Why did you perform the good works? Good works that please my Father are always focused on sincerely trying to improve the well-being of another. Was it done with love? If you performed a lot of good works and deeds but didn't do them out of love, then you will gain nothing."

In one of my teachings I told my disciples, "Love your enemies, do good to them, and lend to them without expecting to get anything back. Then your reward will be great, and you will be sons of the Most High, because he is kind to the ungrateful and wicked." (Luke 6:35 NIV)

Without Love, good deeds will not benefit the one who does them. You must have a Godly motive in your heart, and it must be done with Love.

Now you know the criteria I will test your works by. When we meet at the judgment rewards ceremony, I will conduct only one test:

The test that I will conduct on good deeds and works will determine your rewards.

Journalist:

What do you mean, "test"? I thought the three criteria were the test. What other test is there?

Jesus:

I gave you the three criteria by which your good words and deeds will be tested. The actual test will be done **by fire.**

The fire will test the quality of each believer's work. If what you have built survives, you will receive your reward. **If it is burned up, you will suffer loss;** you yourself will be saved, but only as one escaping through the flames. (I Corinthians 3:11-15)

Your works will be **tested by fire.** I will reward you for all that withstands the fire, and the opportunity to reign with me will be granted.

Get ready—I am coming soon! My reward is with me, and I will give to everyone according to what he has done. (Revelations 22:12)

Journalist:

How could I lose in heaven?

Jesus:

Many of my believers do not believe or understand that you may suffer the loss of your entire Christian career because you didn't have clean motives in your heart. You may have lacked love or done deeds to gain attention. If your motive was not correct, you could suffer loss. *"If it is burned up, **he will suffer loss**; he himself will be saved, but only as one escaping through the flames."* (I Corinthians 3:15 NIV)

You will escape into heaven with few or no rewards. You must be careful and sincere so that you do not lose what you have worked for but be rewarded fully.

I would like to share with you a story I told my disciples 2000 years ago. It reflects on my Father's expectations of His Children. May I share it? It'll only take a moment.

Journalist:

Yes, I'm curious to hear it.

Jesus:

This happened when I was leaving Jericho on my way to Jerusalem the last few days prior to being crucified. I taught the large crowd traveling with me about the **parable of the 10 minas.** In my day, a minas was equal to about three months' salary for the average worker. 10 minas would be about **two-and-one-half years' average wages.**

There was a nobleman who was scheduled to travel to a far-off country where he was to be made king, receive a kingdom, and, after receiving it, he would return.

The nobleman called ten different servants to him and gave them each about two-and-one-half years' salary; he said to them, *"Put this money to work until I come back."* And then he left.

He went to the far-off country, to his own people, but they didn't want him. They didn't receive him with favor. They hated him, formed a delegation, and conspired against him. They said they didn't want this man to be their king. But the nobleman was made king and, afterwards, returned home. Upon arrival, he sent for the ten servants he had given the two-and-one-half years' wages to *in order to find out what they had gained with it.*

The **first servant** said, "**Sir,** Your two-and-one-half years' wages has earned an additional two-and-one-half years of more money." The Master replied, *"Well done, my good servant. Because you have been trustworthy in a very small matter, take charge of ten cities."*

The **second servant** said, Sir, "Your two-and-one-half years of wages has earned one-and-a-quarter years' more money." The Master replied, *"Good work. Take charge of five cities."*

Then **another servant** came and said, "Sir, here is your

two-and-one-half years of wages you gave me. *I have kept it laid away in a handkerchief. I was afraid of you, because you are a hard man. You take out what you did not put in and reap what you did not sow."*

This servant used the excuse of being afraid of the Master, but he wasn't really afraid of the Master. If he had been afraid, he would have put the money in the bank so it could have at least gained interest.

Instead he completely ignored and failed to respond to the nobleman's command of, **"*Put this money to work, until I come back.*"** He kept it laid away in a cloth.

The Master replied to the servant, *"I will judge you by your own words, **you wicked servant!** You knew, did you, that I am a hard man, taking out what I did not put in, and reaping what I did not sow? Why then didn't you put my money on deposit, so that when I came back, I could have collected it with interest?' Then he said to those standing by, "Take his mina away from him and give it to the one who has ten minas." "Sir," they said, "he already has ten!" He replied, "I tell you that to everyone who has, more will be given, but as for the one who has nothing, even what he has will be taken away.*

*"But those enemies of mine who did not want me to be king over them—**bring them here and kill them in front of me.***'"* (Luke 19:22-26 NIV)

CHAPTER 14

JUDGMENT FOR UNBELIEVERS

Journalist:

Jesus, you said there were two judgments, but you've explained only one. When and what is the second judgment for?

Jesus:

The second judgment is the resurrection of **the dead.** My Father and I refer to unbelievers as **"the dead,"** because you are dead to God, while physically alive on earth.

The dead are those who choose not to believe, obey, and love me and my Father's commands. When they die, in the twinkle of an eye, they will be ushered to Hades to be in torment, pain, and anguish, as I described in the story of the rich man and Lazarus.

The judgment of the dead will occur **at the end of ages. This is why** I told you to go and testify to the people that whoever believes in me will receive remission of sins.

The first death for all unbelievers is physical death, in which their soul goes directly to Hades to wait in torment until the time for the resurrection of the dead. Their sins were not forgiven.

At the resurrection of the dead from Hades, the souls of the un-believers will appear before me and my righteous saints, at the Great White Throne Judgment. This is the actual judgment of the unbe-lievers. When the names of the unbelievers are not found written in the **Book of Life,** their souls are judged for their second death, which is **"The Lake of Fire,"** as I described in Revelations 20:10-15. This will become their destination for all of eternity.

Those of you who claim to be my followers but are selectively choosing to believe and abide by some, but not all, of my teachings and instructions, are lost. My Father loves you dearly, but your failure to obey and love me and my teachings seals your eternal destination.

You are fooling yourself into believing you are God's Children. Your name is not written in the Book of Life, and, if you do not repent of your sins and accept me as your Lord and Savior and exchange your life for the life I offer in the kingdom of heaven, you are dead to God and destined to spend eternity in the Lake of Fire, designed for Satan and the evil angels.

Journalist:

Is there any way we can be certain that our names are written in the Book of Life?

Jesus:

Yes, there is. Only those who actually do the will of my Father in heaven will enter. Whoever does the will of my Father in heaven are my brother and sister and mother.

Today, there are many people calling themselves "Christians" who knowingly are living with sin in their lives. You are fooling your-selves by thinking my Father doesn't mind a few small sins. Many people have compromised their soul by following this lie! Their own hearts deceive them. My Father God and sin cannot coexist together.

"Not everyone who says I am a Christian and not everyone who cries out to me 'Lord! Lord!' will enter the Kingdom of Heaven. On judgment day many will say to me, 'Lord! Lord! We prophesied in your name and cast out demons in your name and performed many miracles in your name.' But I will reply, 'I never knew you. Get away from me, you who break God's laws.'" (Matthew 7:21-23)

My Father and I love you and want to spend eternity with you. Right now, you can choose to change your heart and mind before you die or before I come to get my believers. All you need to do is **repent** of your sins and believe in your heart that I am who I said I am and ask me to be your Savior.

Your belief will determine your eternal destination.

The truth is that you must make the correct choices now, today, because there are **no** second chances in eternity. Once you die, **it's final.**

It is your choice; I am coming soon! My reward is with me, and I will give to everyone according to what he has done.

Thank you.

My hope and prayer is that this book has helped you get to know Jesus and Father God. I look forward to hearing your testimony and or feedback you may have regarding this book.

If this book has blessed you please consider giving this book as a gift to someone who is seeking to know the truth about God.

AUTHOR'S FINAL WORD

I AM AN EXAMPLE of the abundance of grace and mercy that God has extended and shown to those who were sinners and those who were His enemies. Because we have believed in Jesus and all that He is, we have become Children of the Most High God.

When I was young, I was raised in a strict, Bible-believing Church and made plans to be a Pastor and work for God, but I ended up running away from Him. I served another god—the god of pleasing myself and, later on in life, of pleasing the family that God blessed me with. Instead of putting God first in my life, I chased the definition of success defined by the companies I worked for. I put all the priorities of this world ahead of God.

At the age of 52, after spending most of my life pursuing prosperity, fame, earthly possessions, and pleasing my selfish desires, God finally broke me down enough so I would listen to Him.

I had just gone through a divorce, ending a 31-year marriage. My purpose for living life had vanished; I was a total failure to God, my family, and now my word. Everything I had lived for, I had failed to attain. I was broken spiritually and financially.

After 40 years of going in circles in the wilderness, I finally came to my senses and asked myself, "Is this the life my mother taught me to live? Is this the life I envisioned to serve for God? Is my life pleasing to God?" The answer was **no** to all the questions. It was obvious I had lived my life making decisions based on what **I wanted to do** and not involving God in any of my plans. I thought about coming back to God, but wondered if He would even allow me to enter His kingdom after living a terrible, sinful lifestyle for 40 years.

So I began to search the Bible to see what God said about such a sinful person. I read that Jesus loved me so much that He came to Earth as God in the flesh and died for me, so that my sins would be forgiven if I confessed them to God. Jesus said that, no matter what sins I had committed, He would forgive me—even stealing, lying, adultery, homosexuality, pornography, divorce, hating and mistreating people, and even not loving God and being obedient to His teachings and structures of creation. No matter what—all the sin I committed, God would forgive me as long as I turned from my wicked ways, repented, and sought to please Him.

Thirteen years ago, with a heart full of remorse, shame, and sorrow, I knelt down on my living room floor. I put my cigarette out and pushed my glass of scotch and water away. Without knowing how to pray, I prayed a little prayer. I asked God to forgive all my sins that I could remember and all those that I couldn't remember, and accept me just the way I was. I pleaded with God not to turn me away because I had been in the pig pen of life, but to cleanse and wash me with the blood of Jesus, so I would be clean to serve Him. I was willing to do anything, as long as he would allow me to become His son. I asked God for His Holy Spirit to come into me and give me the strength to live and do His will.

I began to tell God that I was not worthy to be a son in His kingdom, but before I could say anything else, I felt this big, strong, warm arm slide around me. I had never felt that kind of warmth before. The Holy Spirit of God was all over me. God accepted me before I could complete the sentence. I was free of sin—it was like riding on the warm feathers of an eagle's wing.

God said, "I have washed you and cleansed you in the blood of Jesus. I put clean clothes on you and have shod your feet. You are my son. **I am** with you. I have sealed you with the seal of the Holy Spirit, who will always be with you and will teach you all things.

"You must love me, obey me, and always walk in my ways. I'll never hurt you, and I'll never leave you. You will become a disciple and teach others the **Good News about me** and how to become disciples. I will be with you until the end of time."

The time has come to fall into a deep, loving relationship with Jesus. Remember what He told you: *"Behold, I am coming soon! My reward is with me, and I will give to everyone according to what he has done."* Revelations 22:12

Thank you.

If this book has blessed you please consider giving this book as a gift to someone who is seeking to know the truth about God.

Contact us about buying these books at a discount to use as an evangelistic tool to win souls for Jesus.

And tell others about this book and the other books written by Author Danny Clifford:

> *Behind Enemy Lines: Saved by a Secret Weapon*
> *Last Call*
> *Who Do People Say I Am?*
> *All In* (Available in December 2015)
> Our email is: **http://www.heartandsoulministriesinc.com**

God has anointed me as an Evangelist. As I go about teaching the "Good News Gospel of Jesus," the Holy Spirit will use me as He wills. What-ever gift the Holy Spirit needs, at the moment while I am ministering, He may use me or someone else to accomplish what God the Father wants done.

I am available and would love to come and share with you and your Church *the teachings* that the Holy Spirit has *put in our hearts to minister* for the *Church,* these **last days.**

Michelle, my beautiful wife and best friend, is anointed by the Holy Spirit of God with the gift of prophesy and the gift of a beautiful voice and spirit that brings a group of people—to a state of worshipping God.

Michelle, according to her work schedule, would also love to come and fellowship with you. She absolutely loves to please God—she loves to serve Him.

We wait with great expectation for you to contact us to come and assist you in winning souls for the kingdom of heaven and making disciples for Christ Jesus, as God intended and designed His **Five-fold ministries** to operate in Church. Contact us today.

Our email is: **http://www.heartandsoulministriesinc.com**

Royalties from our books and all donations are donated to our ministry, **Heart and Soul Ministry.** 100 % of all donations are used to support spreading the "Good News of Jesus."

Heart and Soul Ministry is a 501 C 3 non-profit ministry that is devoted to making people of all nations, **disciples for Jesus.**

All donations are tax deductible.

May God bless you as you grow and do the Fathers Will.

98643070R00071

Made in the USA
Columbia, SC
03 July 2018